MATTHEW

by
ARTHUR K. ROBERTSON

MOODY PRESS
CHICAGO

© 1983 by
THE MOODY BIBLE INSTITUTE
OF CHICAGO

Library of Congress Cataloging in Publication Data

Robertson, Arthur K.
  Matthew.

  Bibliography: p. 167.
  1. Bible. N.T. Matthew—Commentaries. I. Title.
BS2575.3.R56 1983   226'.207   83-13202
ISBN 0-8024-0233-X

1 2 3 4 5 6 7 Printing/LC/Year 88 87 86 85 84 83
Printed in the United States of America

CONTENTS

To Linda,
my sweetheart, my best friend, and my wife.
Her love, companionship, and consistent support made this
book possible.

INTRODUCTION

I. Importance of the Book

The prominence of the gospel of Matthew is highlighted by its position as the first book in the New Testament. Renan called it "the most important book in the world" and Goodspeed "the most successful book ever written." The frequency with which it was quoted by Christian writers in the second century showed it to be their favorite gospel. Wilkenhauser stated that "in the time of Irenaeus the Church and Christian literature were more deeply influenced by the Gospel of Matthew than by any other New Testament book."[1] Tasker relates:

> It became known as the "ecclesiastical" Gospel, because it provided the Church with an indispensable tool in its threefold task of defending its beliefs against attacks from Jewish opponents, of instructing converts from paganism in the ethical implications of their newly-accepted religion, and of helping its own members to live a disciplined life of fellowship based on the record of the deeds and words of their Lord and Master which they heard read week by week in the orderly and systematic form provided by this evangelist. In short, the Gospel of Matthew served as an apology, a handbook of instruction, and a lectionary for use in Christian worship.[2]

II. Uniqueness of the Book

Matthew is unique in providing the necessary bridge spanning the 400 silent years between the close of the Old Testa-

---

1. R. V. G. Tasker. *The Gospel According to Matthew*. (Grand Rapids: Eerdmans, 1960), 17.
2. Ibid., 18.

ment canon with Malachi and the fuller revelation of God provided in the Person and work of Jesus Christ. An effective bridge between two eras must contain essential characteristics of both periods to make the spiritual and conceptual transitions possible. Matthew does that by showing the genealogical relationship between Jesus Christ and the Old Testament messianic line, and by quoting directly from the Old Testament fifty-three times and making at least seventy-six allusions to it from twenty-five different books. Eighty-nine of those quotes or allusions were spoken by Jesus. On four occasions He used the Old Testament when speaking of His passion (Matt. 26:31, 54, 56; 27:9).

In presenting his unique emphasis, Matthew brings together several lines of seemingly contradictory Old Testament prophecies. Messiah would be fully human and heir to the throne of David (Isa. 9:7; Matt. 1:1), yet He would be God Himself (Isa. 9:6; Mic. 5:2; Matt. 1:23). Messiah would die (Ps. 22:15-16; Isa. 53:12; Matt. 27:38), yet He would reign on earth (2 Sam. 7:13; Isa. 9:7; Matt. 25:31-34). Jesus Christ, the unique Person of the universe, perfect humanity and undiminished deity united in one Person, came, died for the sins of many, but will come again to reign as Lord and Savior.

Matthew includes a number of events left out of the other gospels: Joseph's vision of Mary's virgin conception; the visit of the wise men to worship Christ; the escape of the holy family to Egypt; Herod's slaughter of the infants at Bethlehem; Pilate's wife's dream about Jesus Christ; Judas's death; the saints resurrected at the crucifixion; the false testimony of the tomb guards after the resurrection; and the baptismal formula in the Great Commission to go into all the world. In addition, Matthew includes ten parables not found elsewhere: the tares sown in the wheat field; the hidden treasure; the pearl of great price; the fish net; the unmerciful servant; the laborers in the vineyard; the two sons; the marriage of the king's son; the ten virgins; and the parable of the talents. Three miracles are found only in Matthew: the two blind men; the dumb demoniac; and the coin in the fish's mouth. Perhaps because he had been a publican, Matthew includes an emphasis on the dangers of money not found in the other gospels: the parable of the unmerciful servant who owed 10,000 talents, and that of the laborers hired for a penny a day; the sum of money paid by the priest to keep the guards quiet about the resurrection; and the thirty pieces of silver that Judas flung into the Temple before hanging himself.

III. THEME AND PURPOSE OF WRITING

The author states that his purpose is to present the "book of the genealogy of Jesus Christ, the Son of David, the Son of Abraham" (1:1), that is, to show that Jesus is the Messiah, the rightful heir to the throne of David, the king of the nation Israel. To do that, Matthew picks up the genealogy of the Messiah where Ruth 4:22 left off with David and traces it back to Abraham. He then organizes the material to show that the Messiah discharged the calling for which He came into the world. The name *Jesus* means "Savior" and the name *Christ* means "Anointed One," or "Messiah." Hence, Matthew is interested in showing that Jesus, the Messiah, had a mission, a foreordained purpose, and a design for His life. He came "to serve, and to give His life a ransom for many" (20:28). The disciples of Christ were to go and make disciples of all nations (28:19). The King was foreordained to come, minister, die, be resurrected from the dead, and come again to reign on earth. Jesus Christ the crucified would one day be Jesus Christ the conqueror and establish the messianic kingdom.

IV. RELATIONSHIP TO THE OTHER GOSPELS

The first three gospels of the New Testament are more similar and, therefore, set apart in content from the fourth gospel. All but fifty verses of the gospel of Mark are found in the gospels of Matthew or Luke. Of the 1,068 verses in Matthew, 500 are like those found in Mark. Of the 1,149 verses in Luke, 320 resemble Mark. The similarities of these gospels represent a common goal and reflect the use of common subject matter. Hence, they are called the *synoptic gospels,* or the gospels that are "seen together." Matthew emphasizes Jesus as the Messiah-King, whereas Mark emphasizes the servant office of Jesus, and Luke places greater emphasis on Jesus' humanity. The gospel of John, as the fourth gospel, places greatest emphasis on the deity of Jesus Christ. The elements stressed in each of the gospels are found in a less-pronounced manner in the others.

Some theologians have postulated the existence of a *Q* document as a source for the common materials found in the synoptics. *Q* stands for *Quelle,* German for "source." Since history has failed to produce evidence for such a document, most conservative scholars reject that theory. It must be stressed that although the Holy Spirit could have used such a resource for the authors to follow (cf. Luke 1:1-4), it was not necessary because He Himself served as the ultimate common unifying source (cf. John 14:26).

V. AUTHORSHIP OF THE GOSPEL

None of the gospel writers identified themselves in their writings, but from earliest times, Matthew was recognized as the author of this gospel. A fragment from a lost work of Papias, Bishop of Hierapolis in Phrygia, about A.D. 130, is the earliest evidence. Papias, relates Bruce, "lovingly collected and recorded what remained of oral tradition handed down by those who had seen and heard the Lord in person. He wrote five volumes called an *Exegesis of the Dominical Oracles,* which is not known to be extant. His work was quoted by various Christian writers of subsequent generations. Among those was Eusebius, who, in the third book of his *Ecclesiastical History,* ascribed to Papias the statement that "Matthew compiled the oracles (logia) in the Hebrew speech, and everyone interpreted them as best he could."[3] Those oracles were the words and the works of Christ. Justin

---

3. F. F. Bruce. *St. Matthew* (Grand Rapids: Eerdmans, 1970), 3.

Martyr, the early Christian apologist, A.D. 100-165, used the gospel of Matthew in support of his arguments. Eusebius himself stated that Matthew committed to writing the gospel as he had proclaimed it. Irenaeus, A.D. 175, stated that "Matthew also issued a written Gospel among the Hebrews in their own dialect, while Peter and Paul were preaching in Rome and laying the foundations of the church."[4] Jerome stated that the converted tax collector Matthew was the first to compose a gospel of Christ.

Matthew Levi, employed as a publican by the despised Roman Empire to collect taxes from his fellow Jews, must have been disliked by his countrymen. Other than his early profession, his call to Christ, and witness to other publicans and sinners at a dinner party at which Jesus was the guest of honor (Matt. 9:9-11), little is known of him. The last mention of Matthew is found in the list of apostles gathered in the upper room awaiting the Day of Pentecost (Acts 1:13).

Some have thought, because of the statements by church Fathers, that Matthew must have written the gospel in Aramaic and that it was later translated into Greek. His training as a tax collector would have enabled him to write in Aramaic, the Hebrew dialect of that period, or in Greek, the common language of the Roman world. Although his writing in Aramaic is possible without bringing into question the doctrine of inspiration, there is *insufficient* internal evidence to support the contention. As Tasker states, "most modern scholars find it very difficult to believe that our Gospel of Matthew is a translation of an Aramaic document. It bears the marks of an original Greek composition."[5]

VI. DATE AND PLACE OF WRITING

Because Matthew speaks of the destruction of Jerusalem as a future event, and history points to A.D. 70 as the date for that event, Matthew must have been written before A.D. 70.

---

4. Merrill C. Tenney. *The New Testament: An Historical and Analytic Survey* (Grand Rapids: Eerdmans, 1960), 151.

5. Tasker, 13.

The testimony of Irenaeus would place the writing during the time of Nero while Paul and Peter were in Rome, about A.D. 50-60.

Antioch of Syria has been suggested as the place of writing, although that cannot be established with certainty.

VII. INSPIRATION AND CANONICITY

Care must be taken to discern the differences between inspiration, authority, and canonicity. Divine inspiration is the means by which God communicated His revelation to man. The books of the Bible were *God-breathed,* that is, they were breathed out of God's mind into the minds of the authors (2 Tim. 3:16). The minds of the writers were "carried along" by the Holy Spirit (2 Pet. 1:21) in the writing of the Scriptures. God used Matthew's personality, eyewitness experiences, education, and possibly other resource materials available to write this gospel. The book bears the unique attributes of the human author. Because it was inspired when written, the book of Matthew is the Word of God, and therefore, authoritative.

Matthew, both internally by its contents and externally by its effects on men, early was proved as inspired. However, it was not until the fourth century that the church was sufficiently organized to see the need to make a formal statement concerning which books had been recognized as inspired. That formal recognition by church councils was called *canonization.* The word *canon* means "reed" or "measuring rod." Hence, the canon of Scripture was to be the measuring rod for the faith and practice of Christians. The Council of Laodicea in A.D. 363, the Third Council of Carthage in A.D. 397, and the Council of Hippo in A.D. 419, all had Matthew at the head of their lists of canonical literature.

VIII. TEACHINGS OF JESUS

As the greatest teacher of all time, Jesus "astonished" His hearers, (7:28; 22:33). To illustrate His thoughts, He used miracles and various teaching devices. His miracles were employed in three ways: first, as attention-getters called *wonders;* second, as displayers of might, called *powers;* and third, as pointers or *signs* of spiritual truth. Although every miracle was intended to teach a spiritual truth, some observers never proceeded beyond the stage of wonderment and missed the highest impact intended by the sign.

The parable was a device created by Jesus for teaching purposes. Only a limited form was used in the Old Testament. The word *parable* comes from the Greek meaning "to lay alongside of" and refers to how Jesus took a physical truth and laid it alongside a spiritual truth to illustrate and confirm that spiritual truth. For example, by the parable of the sower Jesus' disciples were made to understand why some did not believe in Him. In the physical realm, seed sown in poor soil does not produce; so also, seed sown in poor spiritual soil does not produce (Matt. 13:1-23). Parables were always connected with the ordinary circumstances of daily life and were told in an understandable, easy-to-remember manner.

The epigram was a terse, pungent saying that would stick like a barb in the mind of the hearer, as in the Beatitudes (Matt. 5:3-12) or the famous statement, "He who has found his life shall lose it" (Matt. 10:39).

On occasion Jesus used the argument as an effective device, but He always appealed to Scripture for His base, and always argued for the benefit of His hearers (Matt. 22:15-45).

Like the rabbinical schools of His day, Jesus employed the effective use of questions and answers (Matt. 9:5; 16:25; etc.), both encouraging questions and sometimes asking them to make His point.

Object lessons such as little children illustrating humility or a withered fig tree illustrating the results of fruitlessness were poignant teaching devices.

IX. RELEVANCE FOR TODAY

The gospel of Jesus Christ is relevant to every age. The needs of man and the plan of God have not changed. The gospel of Matthew encourages its readers to appreciate the ministry of Christ as the fulfillment of a divinely conceived plan. It encourages Christians to appreciate their Jewish heritage and stresses the relevance of the gospel to the entire world. Whereas Israel, as the depository of God's revelation, was to be a lighthouse set on a hill, Christians are to go into all the world, teaching and baptizing in the name of the Father, the Son, and the Holy Spirit.

X. Outline of the Book

This book may be outlined in a number of different ways, depending on the nature of the study.

GEOGRAPHICAL OUTLINE

A geographical outline would suggest a fourfold division of Matthew:

> Introduction   1:1—4:11
> The Galilean Ministry   4:12—18:35
> The Perean Ministry   19:1—20:34
> The Climax in Judea   21:1—28:20

The Galilean Ministry, those activities of Christ taking place in what was considered the province of provincial and uncultured Jews, the one north of Judea that contained such locations as the Sea of Galilee and the towns of Capernaum, Cana, and Nazareth. Here Jesus performed most of His miracles and found His greatest acceptance.

The Perean Ministry included His activities in that region beyond Jordan and the Dead Sea, which touched the eastern borders of Samaria and Judea. As in Galilee, this was mainly a Jewish sector, country people, with some Gentile villages scattered within the area. The book of Matthew emphasizes the *teaching* of Jesus during this period of ministry as He approached the climax of His life on earth.

The Climax in Judea brought the gospel to a passionate and glorious close. Judea was the largest province containing the "purist" Jewish stock. The prominent religious leaders and the Jewish aristocracy resided there. Towns such as Bethany, Bethlehem, and Jerusalem provided the setting for the final rejection, death, and resurrection of Jesus.

DISCOURSE OUTLINE

Another often-used method of outlining the gospel of Matthew divides it into the six great discourses found in the book, noting the narrative sections between them:

Background 1:1—2:23
Narrative 3:1—4:25
First Discourse: Sermon on the Mount 5:1—7:29
Narrative 8:1—9:34
Second Discourse: Instruction of the Disciples
    9:35—11:1
Narrative 11:2—12:50
Third Discourse: Parables about the Kingdom 13:1-52
Narrative 13:35—17:27
Fourth Discourse: On Humility and Forgiveness 18:1-35
Narrative 19:35—22:46
Fifth Discourse: Condemnation of Religious Leaders
    23:1-39
Sixth Discourse: Olivet Discourse 24:1—25:46
Narrative 26:1—28:20

The narrative sections show the development of Jesus' claims through His words and works, the growth of hostility toward Him, and the ultimate fulfillment of His mission. The discourse sections explain the nature and character of the kingdom of God—when it will come and what it will be like.

THEMATIC OUTLINE

A thematic outline, which is followed through the text of this commentary, attempts to demonstrate the purpose of the author's writing. Although conservative Bible scholars find much unanimity concerning the unique qualities of the book and its basic theme, when we come to an outline we are confronted with many different possibilities. The outline given

here and developed in detail throughout the text is an attempt
to remain true to the clearest thematic divisions of the text:

Preparation of the King   1:1—4:11

Program of the King: His Words and Works
4:12—25:26

Passion and Resurrection of the King   26:1—28:20

1

THE KING'S PREPARATION

I. PREPARATION OF THE KING (1:1—4:11)

This section links Jesus Christ with the Old Testament, unmistakably identifying Him as the Messiah and showing how He was prepared for His ministry.

A. GENEALOGY OF THE KING (1:1-17)

Rampant claims of false messiahs and the disparaging remarks of Christ's critics about His origins (cf. Matt. 13:54-58) dictated that Matthew establish His royal genealogy. Matthew stresses the relationship of Jesus Christ to the two most significant individuals in Jewish history: David, the Jews' greatest sovereign who received the promise "Your house and your kingdom shall endure before Me forever" (2 Sam. 7:12-16); and Abraham, the father of their nation, who received the promise "In your seed all the nations of the earth shall be blessed" (Gen. 22:18). In verse 1, which is a caption for both the next sixteen verses and the rest of the gospel, Matthew stresses Messiah as Sovereign over Messiah as Savior, placing David before Abraham (cf. Matt. 10:5-6; 15:24). The legitimacy of the claims of Jesus Christ to the offices of king and Savior are secured. Levitical laws of inheritance did not necessarily include every generation, hence, some names are omitted.

Three divisions, containing fourteen, fourteen, and thirteen names separate the genealogy into well-known periods of history. Verses 1-6 cover the period from Abraham to David, the time of the patriarchs and Judges. These verses list the

names of significant laity and emphasize the covenant promises for the nation and the land. In uncharacteristic Jewish
fashion, four women are mentioned. Three were Gentiles and
three were guilty of adultery. Tamar the Canaanite's story is
found in Genesis 38:11-30; Rahab of Jericho in Joshua
2:1-21; 6:22-25; Ruth the Moabitess (of whom nothing evil is
recorded) in the book of Ruth; and Bathsheba, the wife of
Uriah the Hittite is found in 2 Samuel 11:1—12:25. Every
name in this section of the genealogy is recorded in the Old
Testament and had rich meaning to God's covenant people,
awakening hope and visions of glory. This section gives us the
origin of David's house.

The second division of fourteen names (vv. 7-11) is the
period of the monarchy, from David to the deportation of
Judah to Babylon. Covenants dealing with the throne and the
holy city are emphasized, while Israel experienced its greatest
glory and deepest moral tragedy. Every name listed is in-
scribed in the Old Testament, representing the best and worst
of spiritual leadership. Even though some kings were royal
failures, God kept His promises. Jehoshaphat, Hezekiah, and
Josiah represented spiritual revival, whereas Rehoboam,
Ahaz, and Manasseh pictured the tragedy of apostasy leading
to captivity. The *rise* and *decline* of David's house took place
during this period.

A hierarchy of priests is recorded in the third division of
thirteen names (vv. 12-17). This was the longest period of
spiritual drought for the covenant nation, beginning with the
Babylonian captivity and culminating in the glorious fulfillment of Jehovah's promises in the birth of Christ. After the
captivity, a person who claimed priestly prerogatives was required to prove priestly descent (Neh. 7:63-64). The first three
names, Jeconiah, Shealtiel, and Zerubbabel, are recorded in
the Old Testament; the others, though apparently kept by
strict family records, lived after the close of the Old Testament canon. A new covenant had been given, emphasizing the
heart (Jer. 31:31). Verse 17 provides a climax to the entire
genealogy, showing how the promises to David's house are

eclipsed by the amazing Person and work of the King.

Note that the genealogy, as all life, begins and ends with Jesus Christ, the Alpha and the Omega (Rev. 1:8), God with us (Matt. 1:23), so that *God's faithfulness* to His promises (24:35) stands bold in contrast to man's historic fickleness (23:37).

Understanding three key words in the text helps to eliminate potential problems: the KJV term *generation* in verse 1 means "genealogy"; the term *son* in the same verse means "kinship"—in this instance, remote descent; and the term *begat* (vv. 2-16) refers to legal ancestry and does not literally mean "the father of," so that Joseph, as the legal father of Jesus, is seen to be the legal descendant of Abraham and David.

In comparing Matthew's genealogy with Luke 3:23-31, some have suggested that Matthew provides the legal line of Messiah through Joseph, His adopted father, whereas Luke provides the natural bloodline of Jesus through Mary, so that few names are duplicated.

B. BIRTH OF THE KING (1:18-25)

In this account of the Savior's birth, Matthew stressed the deity of Jesus Christ. Whereas the genealogy shows Him to be the son of David, His birth shows Him to be the Son of God. The Savior-King was both human royalty and undiminished deity.

Verses 18-21 reveal Joseph's perspective of Christ's virgin conception, which took place during stage two of the three-stage Jewish marriage. In the first stage, Mary had been promised informally to Joseph. This informal "engagement" often took place through an arrangement by parents years before the marriage. Stage two was the betrothal, a public ratification of the engagement making it dissoluble only through death or divorce. The full consummation of the marriage with cohabitation came in the third stage, a year later. Mary had voluntarily submitted to the will of God; Joseph, not knowing of the source of her pregnancy, reluctantly had

decided to divorce her secretly. Had it not been for divine in-
tervention by an angel informing Joseph of how Mary had
conceived and why he should not be afraid of marrying his
betrothed, history would read differently. Adultery was
punishable by death (Deut 22:22). At this juncture, and during the later public ministry, Christ was accused of being an
illegitimate child. In using a play on words, the angel told
Joseph that the child was to be called "Jesus," a common
Jewish name, literally meaning *Savior,* because he would
"save His people from their sins."

In verses 22-23 it is shown that the birth of Christ fulfilled a
particular prediction. Matthew frequently introduces prophetic fulfillment with similar words (cf. 2:15, 17, 23: 4:14;
8:17; 12:17; 13:35; 21:4; 27:9). In the context of Isaiah 7:14,
quoted here, Isaiah was speaking to King Ahaz and predicting
the birth of a royal child as a sign of God's deliverance from a
threat. Isaiah may not have recognized the full implications
of his prophecy, but Matthew saw that the true meaning was
realized, not in the birth of the good king Hezekiah, but in the
birth of Jesus, the virgin's son (according to the Greek
translation of the Old Testament quoted here). Jesus was Emmanuel, "God with us." Divine deliverance would come
through the One who was manifest deity. The purpose of
recording this birth is to show that the Son of Mary is also the
Son of God; that the Savior of mankind is also the Sovereign
of heaven.

Verses 24 and 25 reveal Joseph's response to God's
message. He took unto him his wife (literally, he "took unto
his side"; cf. Gen. 2:21-23). Physical consummation of the
marriage took place after Jesus was born. The genius of the
gospel is here encapsulated in two names, *Emmanuel* and
Jesus. Chapter 1 sets the stage for the amazing events that
follow.

C. WORSHIP OF THE KING (2:1-12)

Chapter 1 shows Jesus deserving of royal honor and
chapter 2 shows that He received it. Even wise Gentiles

recognized Him as King; should the Jews do less?

In verses 1 and 2 we have the arrival of the wise men in Jerusalem in search of the King of the Jews that they might worship Him. The astronomical phenomenon that led them was similar in appearance to a star, yet was probably like the Shekinah glory of God that led Israel in the wilderness. Those wise men were members of a monotheistic oriental caste that believed in prayer, and they were deeply interested in religion and astrology.[1] A widespread desire for a savior was apparent among Gentiles of the period and those men had probably been taught by the Jews of the Dispersion to expect the coming of the Savior, the universal King.

Herod's reaction is disclosed in verses 3-8. This murderous Gentile ruler had gained and held control over Palestine from 37-4 B.C. and was acknowledged by Rome, if not by Israel, as king of the Jews. Now, in the last year of his life, he panicked when he heard that sages from the East sought the newly born rightful heir to the throne. Stirring his dying energy, he called the Sanhedrin and then the wise men to inform him of the place and the time of Messiah's birth. Micah 5:2 was well known by the Jewish community as giving the place of birth. Matthew paraphrases that prophecy here, stressing the nature of the King as sovereign shepherd rather than the place of birth as Micah did. The *magi* (wise men) told Herod when the star first appeared and he sent them on their way, deceitfully requesting that they return with a report.

The magis' worship of the King is recorded in verses 9-12. The star reappeared and led them to the child. Note God's use of general revelation (the star) and special revelation (the prophecy) in leading those true seekers to Christ. The gifts offered were known to the Jews, having been used in their worship: gold in the Temple and Temple furniture; frankincense, pure incense with the meal offerings (Lev. 2:1-2), and myrrh in the composition of anointing oil (Ex. 30:22-33). Origen suggested that the magi brought gold as to a king, myrrh as to

1. William Hendriksen. *Exposition of the Gospel According to Matthew* (Grand Rapids: Baker, 1975), 150.

one who was mortal, and incense as to God. The gifts could have provided financial support for the family during a period of unemployment for Joseph. God warned the wise men not to go back to Herod and they returned home by another route.

The early church saw the visit of the magi foretold in Isaiah 60:3, and the festival commemorating their visit came to be known as Epiphany. That event took place at least forty days after the visit of the shepherds recorded in Luke 2:1-20. Matthew stresses his own theme and leaves out Luke's account of the shepherds and includes the honored wise men who offered expensive gifts worthy of a king, while the great Herod trembled in fear: that is the gospel of the sovereign Savior.

D. DEPARTURE OF THE KING INTO EGYPT (2:13-15)

In contrast to the magi who searched for the King of the Jews to worship Him, Herod sought the child to murder Him. But for the second time in Matthew's account, an angel conveyed a message from God to protect the child king. Joseph was warned that Herod would attempt to kill the child and that they must flee into Egypt. Joseph immediately obeyed and Matthew uses the event of the trip to show how the Messiah was the enlargement of all that God had done for Israel through Moses. In paraphrasing Hosea 11:1, Matthew shows that he regards Israel as a type of the Messiah (cf. Ex. 4:22). As Pharaoh had attempted to destroy Israel, so Herod was attempting to destroy the Christ; but in both instances Jehovah delivered. Because Christ is a descendant of those delivered out of Egypt, when Israel was called out of Egypt, so also was Christ. Thus, Matthew has good reason to say, "That what was spoken by the Lord through the prophet might be fulfilled, saying, 'Out of Egypt did I call My Son.' " The closeness of Jesus Christ to His people is emphasized in Acts 22:7. As God used Moses to deliver Israel from physical bondage in Egypt, so Jesus would be used for the higher purpose, being called out of Egypt to save mankind from the bondage of sin. The messianic Savior was divinely protected for a sublime purpose.

E. HEROD SLAUGHTERS THE INFANTS (2:16-18)

Herod's well-known wrath, which had frequently caused the Jews to tremble, now brought mothers of Bethlehem to a state of anguish. Every male up to two years of age in the region of Bethlehem was slain—perhaps as many as twenty children. Herod had hoped to kill the King of the Jews. In his account, Matthew used another Old Testament quotation, a figurative passage in Jeremiah 31:15 in which Rachel, the mother of Joseph and Benjamin, is pictured rising from her grave and lamenting the destruction of her descendants being led into captivity by the king of Babylon. A counterpart to her anguish is seen in the grief of the mothers of Bethlehem. Matthew quotes from one verse but was pointing to the entire context in which it was originally written, intending that his readers understand that God by His grace would produce victory out of man's misery and defeat. Jeremiah 31:16 reads, "Restrain your voice from weeping, and your eyes from tears; for your work shall be rewarded." Out of the sorrow of the Babylonian exile would come a disciplined and revived Israel who would rebuild the destroyed cities and bring forth the Branch of Righteousness who would "forgive their iniquity" and "remember their sin no more." So also the sorrow of the Bethlehem mothers was destined in the divine providence to result in great reward. Young children had been the first casualties in the battle with the kingdoms of this world that would end in the death and resurrection of Christ. The Savior would overcome all hatred, sin, and death in His glorious act of redemption.

F. RETURN OF THE KING TO NAZARETH (2:19-23)

That Messiah was born in the royal city of Bethlehem would soon be forgotten, for He would be identified with the lowly estate of the town of Nazareth, where He lived for perhaps twenty-eight years (John 1:45-46; 7:42). The sovereignty of God in protecting His Anointed to accomplish man's redemption is again apparent through the fulfillment of prophecy. On two other occasions God spoke to Joseph that what was spoken through the prophets "might be ful-filled" (v. 23).

When Herod died, an angel spoke to Joseph in a dream, telling him to return to Israel. Joseph had intended to settle in Bethlehem, but while he was traveling God spoke to him again and warned him that Archelaus, the tyrant, ruled as the ethnarch over Judea. Joseph decided to settle in Nazareth in the province of Galilee.

Verse 23 has been a problem for Bible scholars because it seems to indicate that the Old Testament specifically proph-esied that Messiah would be called a *Nazarene,* whereas no such prophecy can be found. Matthew may have been using a play on words and thereby alluding to Isaiah 11:1, where the Hebrew word translated "branch," referring to Messiah, has the same root consonants as *Nazarene.* However, Matthew is thinking of more than one Old Testament passage, for he writes "spoken by the prophets" (plural), not prophet (singular). And he does not add the word "saying" as he often did when quoting a specific passage. It is probable that Matthew is referring to the fact that many Old Testament passages, spoken by numerous different prophets, predicted that the Messiah would be considered of lowly estate (Pss. 22:6-8, 13; 69:8, 20-21; Isa. 49:7; 53:2-3, 8; Dan. 9:26). The identification of Jesus Christ with the town of Nazareth gave Him that lowly estate (2:23; 21:11; 26:71). The eternal King humbled Himself and suffered scorn and rejection (Matt. 12:24; 27:21-23, 63) that He might provide a great salvation determined before creation; a salvation revealed in the Old Testament and guaranteed by His sovereignty (1:21; 18:11).

G. PREACHING OF JOHN THE BAPTIST, WAY PREPARER OF THE KING
   (3:1-12)

Approximately thirty years after the birth of Christ, John the Baptist came to remove the faulty religious debris from the hearts of Jews so the way to their minds would be open to the Person and work of the sovereign Savior. As a road would be prepared for an ancient monarch before he traveled it, so also the hearts of men would be prepared for the coming of the King. In a barren desert region, having little vegetation except an occasional bit of brushwood, John found the perfect environment to illustrate the spiritual barrenness of Israel. He called the people to repent, that is, to have a change of mind toward God and themselves that would result in a confession of personal sinfulness and a recognized need for divine forgiveness. The message was urgent, for the kingdom of heaven, the long-anticipated earthly reign of the Messiah, "was at hand." Matthew quotes Isaiah 40:3 to show that John was the prophesied "Elijah" (cf. Matt. 11:1-14; 17:12; John 1:23).

Both the appearance and diet of John denounced self-indulgence and fit his stern message (cf. Lev. 11:22, 2 Kings 1:8; Zech. 13:4). He was generally recognized as a prophet of God (Matt. 21:26), so the people of Israel flocked into the desert to hear the first *new* word from God in more than four hundred years. Believers confessed their sins and publicly declared their repentance and identification with his movement by allowing John to baptize them. His ministry must have shocked the self-righteous who baptized Gentile proselytes but never suspected their own need for repentance and baptism.

When religious leaders came to John feigning spiritual interest, an apparent guise to enlist his support, he rebuked them. Some Pharisees believed they could attain God's kingdom through the performance of religious activities; Sadducees did not even believe in eternal life, but sought power and possessions through the attainment of religious authority. Just as small snakes that look like harmless dead branches but can bite, cling, and kill, the seemingly harmless religious leaders taught doctrines that had the sting of spiritual death. The "wrath to come" (3:7), which they must face, is the coming judgment of the King (Mal. 4:1-5). Spiritual fruit expected of true repentance is described as justice, mercy, and faith (Matt. 23:23; cf. Gal. 5:22-23). Contrary to popular belief, physical descent from Abraham was declared inadequate for the expiation of sins and entrance into the kingdom of heaven. Spiritual children of Abraham would be raised up from *every nation* to enter the kingdom (Eph. 2:14-18; Rev. 7:9). The "axe . . . already laid" at the root of the tree pictured the imminency of "the wrath to come" for unspiritual Israel and her religious leaders.

Some thought John the Baptist was the Messiah (Luke 3:15), but Matthew shows that John made clear he was not even worthy to be Messiah's slave. For example, John warned of judgment, but Christ would be the Judge; and John's water baptism pointed to a need that Christ's Spirit baptism would fulfill. Spirit baptism prophesied in Joel 2:28-29 and Ezekiel 36:26-27 would first take place on the day of the feast of Pentecost (Acts 1:5, 8, 2:1-4; 11:15-16) and then at the point of conversion for every subsequent believer (1 Cor. 12:13). New spiritual illumination, affections, and strength would result. The baptism of fire goes beyond the gracious positive ministry of the Holy Spirit in illuminating and cleansing (cf. Isa. 6:6-7; Acts 2:3; 1 Pet. 1:7) to speak of the final judgment at the return of Christ to cleanse the earth (2 Thess. 1:7-8; Mal. 3:2; 2 Pet. 3:7). John saw the first and second comings of Christ in proximity. In the fashion of an Old Testament prophet, he "foreshortened" the two comings of Christ and like two great mountains seen from a distance that appear to be close together, Matthew 3:12 supports the thought that fire baptism refers to final judgment at the second coming, when the "grain" (true believers) is placed in the storehouse (John 14:2), and the "chaff" (rejectors) is burned up; that is, they face the everlasting wrath of God (Rev. 20:12-15).

H. BAPTISM OF THE KING (3:13-17)

All Israel had heard of John's plea for repentance. Jesus, too, was called to stand for or against the prophet of God. Only Matthew records that John hesitated when Jesus came to him requesting baptism. John 1:31, 33 assert that John the Baptist did not recognize Him. That could mean that he had not yet recognized the implications of Jesus' ministry, for it is unlikely that the cousins (cf. Luke 1) would not have met previously. During the interview before baptism, John must have realized the purity of Christ in comparison with his own sinfulness, and he naturally balked at a baptism of repentance for One who was sinless. John desired to be baptized by Jesus. Jesus did not deny His superiority to John, but said that John must baptize Him "to fulfill all righteousness," to comply with every righteous requirement and fulfill the Scriptures in which God's commands were enshrined. Levitical law required that a sacrifice be identified with the sacrificer (Lev. 1:4). Christ was being identified with John, the ministry, and the believing remnant as the sacrifice that would be offered for the remnant (Isa. 53:6; Matt. 20:28; 2 Cor. 5:21). The sinless One identified Himself with sinners. That event marked a change from a quiet, peaceful home life in Nazareth to the beginning of a public ministry that would end in the ultimate sacrifice.

The most significant aspect of that account is the authentication of Jesus as Messiah by the voice of the Father in a composite quote from Psalm 2:7 and Isaiah 42:1, passages on which Jesus must have often meditated. Jewish kings were anointed with oil, a symbol of the Holy Spirit's ministry to them and through them (1 Sam. 10:1; 16:13). Thus, as prophesied (Isa. 11:1; 42:1), the Messiah was anointed with the Holy Spirit, who descended upon Him like a dove. He must have the power of the Holy Spirit on His ministry to accomplish His divinely appointed program as the God-man.

Having been publicly identified with the Baptist's message for sinners, authenticated by the voice of the Father, and anointed by the Holy Spirit, Jesus was ready for the final step in preparation for His public ministry.

I. TEMPTATION OF THE KING (4:1-11)

Having been identified with sinners through His baptism, Christ would be tempted "in all things" (Heb. 4:15) and, therefore, be enabled to empathize with sinners. At the threshold of His public ministry, He emphatically demonstrated superiority over Satan; the Messiah would not and could not sin. Inherent in this passage is the glorious promise that victory is certain; the Messiah will establish His kingdom! Immediately after His baptism (cf. "then," v. 1) the Spirit led Christ into the wilderness, where for forty days and nights He apparently prayed and meditated on the Scriptures in anticipation of His mission. Then came the temptations from His "adversary" (the devil, lit., "slanderer"). The first Adam, tempted in the Garden, failed. The Second Adam (1 Cor. 14:45), tested in the wilderness, was victorious.

The three temptations described by Matthew apparently are given in chronological order (cf. Luke 4:1-13) and grow in severity, from the initial temptation to put physical needs ahead of spiritual responsibility; the temptation to prove Himself by disregarding God's physical laws; to the ultimate temptation to receive the kingdoms of this world without first suffering death in the place of sinners. Each quote Jesus used to respond to Satan is taken from the wilderness experience of Israel recorded in Deuteronomy. By saying, "If (lit., "since"; cf. vv. 3 and 6) You are the Son of God," Satan acknowledged the deity of Jesus Christ. In the first temptation Satan suggested that the famished Christ change stones into bread. The error in Satan's suggestion was that material needs are all that are necessary in life. Christ's response by quoting Deuteronomy 8:3 was that abiding in the will of God is the primary need. Every "word that proceeds out of the mouth of GOD" (v. 4) is the "word of the LORD," by which authority all things came to be (Ps. 33:6). Failing in his first attempt, Satan took Jesus to Jerusalem where he suggested that Jesus throw Himself off a 450-foot drop from the outer Temple wall to a bed of sharp rocks. In quoting from Psalm 91:11-12, Satan left out the phrase "in all your ways" (v. 11; cf. John 8:44) and treacherously suggested a misinterpretation of the promise. The psalmist is teaching trust in the Lord in times of testing, not rash disregard for God's natural laws. Principles governing the universe, such as the law of gravity, are reflections of God's character, and Jehovah strongly speaks against arrogant actions in His name (cf. Num. 14:22-23; Ps. 19:13; Dan. 4:28-33; 5:22-23). In His rebuke of Satan, Jesus revealed the correct interpretation of the passage by quoting Deuteronomy 6:16, wherein Moses reminded the Jews, before they entered Canaan, of the lesson of presumptuous failure in the desert (Ex. 17:1-7). They had challenged God and accused Him of misdirection in their lives, jeering, "Is the LORD among us, or not?" Jesus, in His place of wilderness testing, was above Israel's mistake. Christ could not be goaded out of trusting His Father and into pridefully ignoring His natural laws. Christians will sometimes flout God's "laws" while pleading His blessing (cf. Heb. 3:7-11). In the final temptation, Satan offered Christ His rightful heritage—the kingdoms of this world—for returned worship (Ps. 72:8), but without the cross. God has allowed Satan some power in this world (Luke 4:6; Eph. 2:2; 6:12; 1 John 5:19), but ultimate authority and ownership belongs to Him (Gen. 3:15; Ps. 2; Matt. 11:27; 28:18). Satan offered what he did not own. Christ responded by commanding Satan to leave and paraphrased Deuteronomy 6:13-14. The Word is clear; only God is to be worshiped. When anything (even a worthy goal) takes the place of the worship of God, Satan gains control. The kingdom that Christ sought would be lost. Never does the end justify the means. Inherent in this temptation is Satan's acknowledgement that he is defeated; first by the grammatical nature of the conditional particle "if," which in the original Greek connotes a high degree of doubt; and seconded by his immediate departure at Christ's command. The Father showed the Prince of Darkness that the Son was beyond failure. Messiah will triumph and reign (Isa. 9:6-7; Matt. 28:18; Rev. 20:6). Although Satan would be allowed to return and continue his attempts to thwart the work of the Savior (Matt. 13:39; 16:23; 26:36-46), his doom was certain (Rev. 20:10). After the departure of the devil, God's angels ministered to Christ's needs. The sympathetic Savior, having met and defeated every temptation that His disciples would meet (1 John 2:16), provided for them a "way of escape" (1 Cor. 10:13) and victory (James 1:12) through Himself (Matt. 17:18; James 4:7). He was then prepared to offer Himself publicly as Messiah to all who would receive His forgiveness and rule.

2

THE KING'S PREACHING

II. PROGRAM OF THE KING: HIS WORDS AND WORKS (4:12—25:46)

After Matthew identifies Jesus Christ as the Messiah, he reveals what Jesus said and did as He offered the kingdom of heaven to mankind. The program of the King demonstrated a perfectly intergrated balance between *saying* and *doing,* so that observers could both conceptualize and visualize the will of God through the life of Christ.

A. PREACHING OF THE KING (4:12—7:29)

Jesus preached to bring men to repentance. He caused people from all walks of life and all stages of intellectual and moral development to reassess their personal and social values in anticipation of entering His kingdom.

1. *Preaching in Capernaum* (4:12-17)

Possibly a year had passed since the temptation in the wilderness, during which the events recorded in John 2:1—4:42 occurred. Jesus was about to withdraw from Judea for at least two reasons: (1) fulfillment of prophecy (cf. Matt. 2:14-16) and (2) the imprisonment of John the Baptist. Jesus' popularity in Judea was growing so rapidly that if He had not left, He might have prematurely prompted a crisis. Jesus passed through Nazareth but would return (Matt. 13:53-58). Capernaum, the fishing town on the coast of the Sea of Galilee and home of Matthew (9:9), became His headquarters during His Galilean ministry (9:1). There Christ would call His early disciples (John 1:35-42), perform many miracles, attend synagogues, and present several discourses. A garrison

of soldiers was there. It was also a political administration
center located on a trade route with easy access to other
Galilean cities. The words and works of Christ performed
there would produce blessing and judgment. Matthew viewed
Jesus' settlement in Capernaum, where He spent most of His
life, as another fulfillment of prophecy in his paraphrase of
Isaiah 9:1-2, and in the process thwarted the critics who
claimed that Messiah could not be a Galilean. The five locations mentioned probably refer to different sections of
Galilee. The northernmost stretch of what used to be called
Naphtali came to be called *Galilee of the Gentiles* because of
its pagan population. Zebulun and Naphtali were the first of
the conquered tribes to fall to foreign powers and be morally
and religiously influenced by them. These were those "people
who walk in darkness, . . . who live in a dark land" (Isa. 9:2).
That means they were spiritually blind and despondent,
without hope. Darkness is used figuratively in Scripture of
delusion, the blindness of mind and heart (2 Cor. 4:4, 6; Eph.
4:18); depravity (Acts 26:18), and despondency (Isa. 9:2).
Light is the antonym of darkness and refers to learning the
true knowledge of God (Ps. 36:9), living life to God's glory
(Eph. 4:15, 25; 5:14), and gladness and laughter (Ps. 97:11).
It is implied here that Jesus was bringing the message to a
region that John the Baptist had not touched.

2. *Jesus Calls the First Four Disciples* (4:18-22)

There are a number of calls to discipleship and the closely
related apostleship. In John 1:35-51 Christ called Andrew and
most likely John. Andrew brought Peter and John most likely
brought James. Philip and Nathaniel were also added. The
disciples spent time with Jesus but continued their "secular"
occupations. Approximately a year later Peter, Andrew,
James, and John became the Lord's more steady companions
and were made more conscious than ever that they were being
trained for apostleship (that is, to be fishers of men, John
4:18-22). A little later, as recorded in Luke 5:1-11, the
disciples left all and, during the entire precrucifixion period

of Christ's early ministry, said farewell to their occupation as fishermen and followed Jesus permanently. Matthew Levi, the publican and author of this gospel, is called in Matthew 9:9-13. He immediately left his business and followed Christ. Finally, in 10:1-4 is the ultimate formal call of the twelve to discipleship/apostleship. Much has been said about the natural weaknesses and backgrounds of the apostles and how they were gradually transformed by the Holy Spirit into positive testimonies of the grace of God by trusting their lives to the Messiah-King. By means of a concordance the serious student can follow the biblical record of that process.

3. *Preaching and Healing Throughout Galilee* (4:23-25)

With Capernaum as His hub of operation, Jesus·fanned out into the surrounding areas of Galilee. He both preached and taught. Preaching means *announcing* or *proclaiming,* placing an emphasis on the need for making decisions. Teaching indicates *imparting more detailed information* regarding the announcement made. Jesus preached and taught the need to recognize the rule of God over one's own life. He offered a salvation from lesser rulers. Jesus illustrated the all-inclusive nature of that great salvation by healing every kind of illness and infirmity. His miracles confirmed His message (John 14:11) and showed that He was the Messiah who was fulfilling prophecy (Isa. 35:5; 53:4-5; 61:1; Matt. 11:2-6). Demoniacs, epileptics, and paralytics are especially mentioned as exemplary of the inclusive nature of this work. Christ assailed the works of Satan and destroyed his work! News of Jesus' miracles spread to Syria, northeast of Palestine. Although Christ came to the Jews, both Jews and Gentiles came to Him.

4. *The Sermon on the Mount* (5:1—7:29)

This is the King's first discourse recorded in the gospels. It was probably early spring, in the region of Capernaum at a well-known hill designated as "the mountain" (5:1). Jesus had spent the previous night in prayer (Luke 6:12), chosen

His disciples that morning (Mark 3:13-19), and healed many who were sick (Luke 6:17-19). With the newly chosen disciples in the foreground and the less committed in the background, He delivered His most famous sermon. His purpose in that address was infinitely above the mere description of a human standard of morality, serving at least two higher purposes. First, in presenting the character of the awaited kingdom, the expectant Jews were given a lesson in their own moral and spiritual bankruptcy. Christ preached and taught the need for repentance as a prerequisite to entering the kingdom of heaven. Then He described what repentance entailed; second, those who would become committed disciples of the King are given a standard by which to measure their present character and a glimpse at what, by God's grace, they would become (1 John 3:2). That is the standard of holiness Christ requires of all His disciples.

The Sermon on the Mount is the greatest discourse ever given, but it is not the essence of Christianity. Aside from the truth of the divine Person and redeeming work of Christ, it would cause us "bewilderment and despair." The atonement is not specifically developed here, but it is inherent in Jesus' words (cf. 5:3-4; 6:12, 14-15; 7:7-11) and developed later in Matthew (cf. 16:16-20; 22:42-45; 25:31-46). Christ was describing the character of His dominion, the kingdom of heaven (5:3, 10, 19-20; 6:10, 33; 7:21). This is the "gospel [good news] of the kingdom" (4:23).

Because of obvious distinctions between the accounts of the sermon found in Matthew and Luke, some, like Tasker, have suggested that the sermon is a compilation of sayings of Christ delivered over an extended period of time. That is unlikely because the context seems to dictate that the sayings were all part of one sermon delivered at one time. Both records begin with "He began to teach" (Matt. 5:2) or "He began to say" (Luke 6:20) and conclude with "When Jesus had finished these words" (Matt. 7:28), and "When He had completed all His discourse" (Luke 7:1). The distinctions are better explained as the result of two independent recorders including or excluding material that best suited their purposes. Luke pictures Christ standing, possibly after He had descended from the mountain to perform His healing ministry (Luke 6:17). Matthew pictures Christ subsequently having re-ascended the mountain and as seated to conduct His teaching ministry (Matt. 5:1).

a. Happiness of Kingdom Citizens: The Beatitudes, (5:1-16)
This section historically has been called the *Beatitudes,* derived from the Latin word *beatitudo,* meaning "happy" or "blessed."

We are told that those who acknowledge Him as Lord and King and display these virtures will receive blessings in part now (1 Pet. 4:14) and fully hereafter (Matt. 5:12). What makes His words so dynamic is that He Himself possesses these qualities in infinite degree. The people were transfixed as Jesus stated that the oft-despised qualities and circumstances are the ones that bring true happiness when they direct us to God. The poor who are blessed are those who see their need for God. So in each beatitude the place of God is the key; He is the source of blessing.

Jesus is not describing eight different classes of people—the poor in spirit, mourners, and so on—but eight interrelated qualities that would take root in His disciples and develop with the life of faith. The earliest sign of God's grace at work in a potential disciple's heart is a consciousness of spiritual poverty that produces an attitude of mourning for sin. As the person longs for God, God will extend salvation to him and the kingdom of heaven will be his. Salvation will bring comfort to his spirit. He will begin to take on the gentle, meek character of his new King. He will not be timid or weak but will hold his strength in abeyance under provocation to accomplish God's purposes. The meek, with his King, will inherit the earth. Christ's righteousness has been imputed to him (2 Cor. 8:9), he will hunger for the expression of that righteousness in his life (1 Pet. 2:2) and be satisfied. Knowing hurt and healing in his own experience, he will be sensitive to

the hurt of others and will attempt to minister to them (2 Cor.
1:4). Showing mercy, he will receive the same in return. By
God's grace he will learn to discern and face truth about
himself and others, and thereby display sincerity without
hypocrisy (cf. Ps. 24:3-5; 1 Tim. 1:5; James 3:17). He also has
the assurance that he will see God. Viewing life from God's
perspective will give him peace that he will desire to share with
others (Eph. 6:15). He is a child of God (John 1:12) and will
face persecution, which when endured, will bring special
reward. Hendriksen concludes, "It is clear therefore that at
least in their general trend the beatitudes follow the actual
course of the development of new life, and that, in a broad
outline, the sequence found here parallels what is found
elsewhere in the sayings and discourses of the Lord."[1]

Persecution of kingdom disciples represents the attitude of
the world toward them. Verses 12-14 describe the effect of the
disciples on the world. Two metaphors, one dealing with *salt*
and the other with *light,* teach that the persecuted disciples,
despised and rejected, are the most positive influence on the
world. Salt has many characteristics, but here the potency of
salt as an antiseptic is primarily in view. It prevents and
retards decay. Believers, exemplifying the character of God,
hinder further moral decay of the image of God in mankind
(cf. 2 Thess. 2:6-7). Light dispels darkness and attracts life to
itself. Christians ought to attract others to Christ. Salt acts
secretly and has a negative quality, whereas light acts openly
and has a positive quality. The two metaphors compliment
each other. *Light* in Scripture indicates a true knowledge of
God (cf. Ps. 36:9); *goodness* indicates righteousness and
truthfulness (Matt. 6:22-23; Eph. 5:8-9); and *joy* indicates
gladness and true happiness (Ps. 97:11; Isa. 9:1-7; 60:19). In
fact, light symbolizes the best there is in learning, love, and
laughter as contrasted with darkness, which symbolizes the
worst there is in dullness, depravity, and despair. Sometimes

---

1. William Hendriksen. *Exposition of the Gospel According to Matthew*
(Grand Rapids: Baker, 1975), 266.

light refers to all the blessings of salvation (Ps. 27:1; Luke 1:77-79).

However, neither the salt nor the light is the private ownership of the disciple. Christ is the true Light and the true Salt. Servants are extensions of their Master; they are "light in the Lord" (Eph. 5:8). True servants of the King are to let their light shine and allow their salt to preserve, produce a thirst for God, and add flavor to life. That is the legacy of the King's disciples to the world.

b. Moral Standards (5:12-48)

Moral laws given by God to Moses for the theocratic kingdom are also applicable to Messiah's reign over the kingdom of heaven. The Savior came not to abrogate or amend the moral laws of the Old Testament but to interpret them accurately and to see them fulfilled (vv. 17-20). One's position in the kingdom is related to his observance of those changeless laws. Mere external observance is contrasted with a sincere response of the heart.

Six times the Lord refers to the rabbinic interpretation by saying, "You have heard it was said," or, "It was said," before contradicting that superficial interpretation with "but I say to you" (vv. 21-48). The sixth commandment has a deeper implication. Brooding anger can lead to murder and, therefore, is wrong. Although degrees of anger are stated, the point is not to split hairs over degrees of sin, but rather to make the basic point that the root of evil is in the heart. Anger is not always wrong (cf. Eph. 4:25). Instead of abiding anger, reconciliation to one's brother is the required antidote.

As hatred is the root of murder, so also is undisciplined desire the root of adultery (vv. 27-32). It is the impure heart that condemns. The tense of the verb "looks" indicates repeated looking to incite longing, not the accidental or incidental look that is not repeated.[2] The suggested amputation

---

2. Oswald J. Sanders. *Bible Studies in Matthew's Gospel* (Grand Rapids: Zondervan, 1975), 31.

of bodily parts is hyperbolic and emphasizes the point that
immoral lust should be dealt with in an emphatic manner. It is
the mind, not the hand, that sins. Divorce is allowed only
when the offending party is guilty of adultery. Obtaining a
divorce to marry another individual and gratify lust breaches
moral law. The nonguilty party in a divorce may be caused to
commit adultery[3] or be exposed to the temptations of adultery[4] (cf. 1 Cor. 7:5-6).

The law of retaliation is discussed in 5:38-42. "Eye for
eye" merely stated that the penalty was to fit the crime (Ex.
21:24). That is a fundamental principle found in all legal
systems of all ages. However, some Pharisees used that law as
a pretext for revenge. The instruction not to resist "him who
is evil" does not mean that disciples should allow the innocent
to suffer wrong if they can help prevent it. Rather, a disciple
should not resist an evildoer with equally evil measures; that
is, he should avoid vindictiveness and never inflict suffering
in a spirit of revenge. Injustice suffered through the legal process should be borne as a burden of love. Christ does not encourage the foolish granting of loans (v. 42). However, a
loan is never to be withheld because of a desire for revenge.
As one has freely received, so should he freely give (2 Cor.
8:9).

Finally, the Savior spoke of the law of love (vv. 43-48). To
excuse himself from the precept to love his neighbor as
himself, the Pharisee interpreted his neighbor to be his fellow
countryman and members of other nations as his enemy. In
contrast, Christ says that disciples must love their enemies
and pray for those who persecute them. God is the example of
such grace. Even pagans can and do show natural affection
for their friends.

c. Religious Motives (6:1—7:6)

Religious actions do not sanctify evil motives. Here Jesus

---

3. Ibid., 33.
4. Hendriksen, 306.

uses six examples of Pharasaic practice that were motivated by selfish, unscriptural reasoning.

Matthew 6:1 serves as an introduction and summary for this entire section. Pietistic practices should be motivated by a desire to honor God, not for the purpose of getting the applause of men. True love of God and trust in Him manifests itself in properly motivated charitable giving, prayer, and fasting. It is incompatible with worry, the worship of manna, or a hypercritical spirit.

Charitable giving (vv. 2-4) is taken for granted (Ex. 23:10-11; Amos 2:6-7) and is to be done privately. Public observation is to be coincidental, not planned (Matt. 5:16). Someday all deeds, good and bad, will be openly declared (10:26-27). Verse 3 suggests that disciples should not keep a record for the purpose of congratulating themselves (cf. 25:37-39).

Proper prayer is addressed in Matthew 6:5-15 (cf. Luke 11:2-4). The Jews characteristically prayed at three times each day (Ps. 55:17; Dan. 6:10). The King is not condemning all public prayer, only ostentatious prayer. The hypocrite is an actor whose prayer is a performance for the applause of the crowd rather than a sincere conversation with God. Sincerity (John 4:24), not secrecy is what Christ desires of His disciples. Meaningless repetitions were a heaping-up of empty phrases, born of a spirit of fear and designed to inform and then to placate the pagan deities (cf., 1 Kings 18:25-29). A true disciple's prayer should be enlightened by an understanding of the character of the King. God knows His servants' needs, but desires to hear their requests. Matthew 6:9-15 presents a model prayer. It is not the Lord's Prayer in the sense that He needed to pray this prayer; as the sinless One, He did not need to request forgiveness (cf. v. 12). Disciples are told to pray "in this manner" or "in this way," not in exactly those words (v. 9a). Here the King gives a model by sharing six prayer principles that pertain to the past, present, and future of His disciples. These principles are petitions related to the Father: (1) that men reverence Him (i.e., His

Name); (2) that His kingdom (i.e., His Lordship) be established on earth; and (3) that His will be as perfectly followed on earth as it is in heaven. Then He speaks of three principles related as petitions for human needs: (1) physical sustenance, (2) spiritual forgiveness, and (3) moral leadership. Listeners recognized that God was the Father of Israel (Isa. 63:16; 64:8) and of individual believers (Pss. 27:10; 68:5; 89:26, 28), but Jesus stressed that God is the Father of those who are forgiven. Only when a disciple has correctly understood how he has been forgiven and is able to forgive others can he have the correct motive for prayer (v. 12; cf. Matt. 18:21-35).

Kingdom fasting is born out of a desire to serve God, not to gain the praise of men (6:16-18). In the believing community, prayer and fasting were often combined (cf. Isa. 58 for a number of different reasons; Lev. 16:29-34; Judg. 20:26; Acts 13:2-3). Here, fasting is supposed to be a sign of humility, but the Pharisees fasted to gain the praise of men, not to prove their sincerity to God.

Covetousness pertaining to property and other material wealth is unbefitting a child of the King (6:19-24). A disciple motivated by true love for the King places everything at His disposal. Treasures acquired solely for personal gain are subject to loss. Wealth in the Orient was perserved in garments, grain, gold, and precious stones. In contrast, the "heavenly treasures" described in the Beatitudes (5:1-12), are tasted now but more fully enjoyed later (1 Pet. 1:4). It is not wrong to make provision for future physical needs, to provide for one's family (1 Tim. 5:18), give to others in need (2 Cor. 8:4, 9), and to support the spread of the gospel (Phil. 4:15-17). But acquisition of material wealth should be for use in God's purposes (1 Cor. 10:31). As the healthy physical eye makes good use of physical light, so a healthy spiritual eye should make good use of spiritual light. A misused spiritual faculty brings disorientation and disaster (cf. 2 Cor. 4:4). Man cannot combine two opposite goals. A misplaced heart and misdirected mind will result in a misaligned will; a will not in line with the King's will.

Unlimited trust is the fifth practice required of a disciple (6:25-34). Lack of trust in the King produces anxiety that results in the substitution of material things for a trusting relationship with God. Such a misplaced trust confuses values and wears down reason. The word used in the original for *anxious* means "being distracted," or in this context, having one's attention divided from the moral will of the King to solve his problems or meet his needs. The disciples are told to "stop being anxious" about their basic needs (v. 25), for anxiety will neither increase the duration nor quality of life. The field lilies to which Christ points as illustrative of God's care over His creation probably refer to all kinds of wild flowers. Using the argument "from the lesser to the greater," verse 30 asserts that if God cares for the least of His creation, how much more will He care for those made in His own image (cf. Rom. 8:31-39). But the disciple is not to be passive in the attainment of either physical (2 Tim. 3:10) or spiritual needs (Phil. 2:12-14). Hence, the injunction to be seeking constantly to fulfill the principles of His kingdom (v. 33). When all other needs are subservient to that principle, all needs will be met. Disciples are to understand that God meets daily needs on a daily basis (1 Cor. 10:13; Heb. 4:16).

A correct motive in making judgment is crucial to a servant of the King (Matt. 7:1-6). It is necessary to discriminate, but to be hypercritical is wrong. "One should avoid saying what is untrue (Ex. 23:1), unkind (Prov. 18:8), and unnecessary (Prov. 11:3)."[5] It is wrong to concentrate on the minor problem in your brother's eye while ignoring the major problem distorting your own vision (cf. Gal. 6:1). A self-righteous, hypercritical spirit causes one to ignore his own major faults while occupying himself with the minor faults of others (Luke 18:9; 1 Cor. 11:28). Such a person has not yet understood himself or the grace of God and is consequently incapable of judging others. His standard for judgment reveals his degree of maturity and, therefore, is the standard by which he is

---

5. Ibid., 357.

judged. That thought, stated in verse 1, is repeated for emphasis in verse 2. Visual obstructions prevent clear vision.

That a form of judgment is necessary is made clear by verse 6. One must discern between dogs, hogs, and brothers. "What is holy" and the "pearls" refers to a knowledge of God. The "dogs" here are not pets, but ravaging, vicious street scavengers. The swine metaphor teaches that some will not only reject the truth, but also despise it and turn on those who share it. God's patience has limits (Prov. 29:1), and His servants are not to spend an inordinate amount of time with rejectors whose "tearing" can sap the energy of the disciples and keep them from the "fields that . . . are white for harvest" (John 4:35).

d. Persistent Prayer Produces Proper Motives (7:7-12)

How can a disciple gain the sensitivity and discretion necessary to make proper judgments without being judgmental; to be critical without being hypercritical; and to be patient without being too patient? The Lord's answer is "ask . . . seek . . . knock." The scale of intensity ascends from the point of initial humbling at which help is requested to the deeper involvement of seeking to the final step of knocking on the door of the King. The present tense is used with each of the verbs and can be translated, "Continue to ask, continue to seek, and continue to knock." The Lord again argues from the lesser to the greater: If an earthly father would take care of His children, how much more would our heavenly Father do for His children? Although the promise specifically applies to the development of character and spiritual maturity, that same concept has other related applications (cf. Luke 11:5-8).

The "golden rule" found in verse 12 summarizes much of the Sermon on the Mount bracketed between 5:17 and 7:12. In 5:17 Christ said that He came not to abolish the law and the prophets, and in 7:12 He summarized how the law and the prophets were fulfilled. The summary begins with "therefore," showing its logical relationship to the preceding context. Because of gratitude for the Father's continuing care, the disciple should love his neighbor as much as he loves himself. An attitude of dependence on God evidenced in persistent prayer will also be evidenced in an attitude of love toward others equal to the love that one has for himself. That love fulfills the law and the prophets and is the prerequisite motivation for all effective prayer (cf. 1 John 3:22). Only as the believer is energized by the Holy Spirit can he experience that love motive (cf. Rom. 8:4; Gal. 5:22-25).

e. Exhortations to Respond to the King's Words (7:13-27)

Three exhortations close Christ's teaching: To seek entrance into the kingdom (vv. 13-14), to beware of false prophets who would deceive men from truth (vv. 15-23), and to obey commandments to avoid calamity (vv. 24-27). Three striking metaphors clarify the contrasting choices: there are two ways, two kinds of fruit, and two kinds of builders. A note of urgency permeates these verses—choose the kingdom or face destruction.

"Enter" (v. 13) introduces the metaphor of the two ways and is here used as a word picture of conversion (cf. Matt. 4:17; 11:28-30). Conversion is prefigured in Isaiah 1:18 and 55:1. Entering the narrow gate is not going to heaven, but is the beginning of the disciple's life on earth. The gate leads to the way that leads to the life. Conversion comes first, then sanctification. The wide gate is the way of the world with its self-indulgence rather than the kingdom way with its inherent restrictions and disciplines (cf. Jer. 21:8). The alternative to the narrow way is "destruction" (v. 13).

"Beware" (v. 15) introduces the second metaphor, which deals with two kinds of fruit (vv. 15-23) and emphasizes alertness to danger. A disciple must distinguish between true and false prophets. False prophets, though disguised, can be known by their fruits. Their character will produce a caricature of real fruit. Their false doctrine is unhealthy and should be rejected as one rejects a diseased tree. Inspect the "fruit" with a possibility of rejecting the tree (2 John 10). False prophets can share biblical principles with others (vv.

21-22) while rejecting the application of those principles to themselves (James 2:14). They will be condemned for not practicing what they preach. Some will even do mighty works in His name (e.g., Judas, Matt. 10:1; 26:24; Rev. 16:14).

"That day" (v. 22) refers to the final judgment, when the King will be the Judge (Matt. 25:31-33; 26:64; 28:18).

"Therefore" (v. 24) introduces the third metaphor, the two builders (vv. 24-27). Because those who enter the kingdom are saved from destruction, they are wise; that is, they have applied the truth of God to their lives. Such kingdom disciples are analogous to a man who built his life on a "rock," a solid foundation. "These words of Mine" (v. 26) are the solid foundation, and by application of the entire Word of God the disciple can build his life on that foundation. To trust Christ's words is to trust His character. Christ is referred to as the Rock in Isaiah 28:16; Romans 9:33; 1 Corinthians 10:4; and 2 Peter 2:6-8. God is said to be the believer's Rock in Deuteronomy 32:15, 18; Psalms 18:2; 89:26; and Isaiah 17:10. The "rain," "floods," and "winds" (vv. 25, 27) that "burst against that house" refer to the many different trials of life (James 1:12; 1 Pet. 1:3-9). The Lord's construction is indestructible (Ps. 127). The foolish man who took the "broad way" and rejected the King did not face extinction, but ultimately faced *destruction,* eternal separation from God. What his life had built failed to merit fellowship with God and he was judged with the words "depart from Me" (v. 23).

f. Reaction to Messiah's Sermon (7:28-29)

Not only did Christ contradict the shallow deceptions and misinterpretations of the scribes and Pharisees, He also used a startling, dramatic, and refreshing method. He was simple but brilliant; He spoke to many critical issues but held to one theme; and He spoke with unique authority (Matt. 5:18, 26; 7:28-29). Instead of quoting other scribes and Pharisees as was typical for a teacher, His authority was from the Father (John 8:26), Scripture (Matt. 4:4, 7), and Himself (5:17;

13:54-55). The people in the crowd were literally "struck out of themselves," or as the *Amplified Bible* paraphrases it, they "were astonished and overwhelmed with bewildered wonder." The verb tense shows that the effect remained for a time. The world has wondered at His words ever since. "And it came to pass" is found four times in Matthew to introduce reaction to what Christ said to the disciples.

3

THE KING'S MIRACLES

B. MIRACLES OF THE KING (8:1—9:38)

Here Matthew records a series of nine unique displays of supernatural power. Because Christ was King, He was able to back up His words with demonstrations of authority. The miracles covering varied spheres of existence are grouped in three sets of three, connected by relevant narratives. They are topically rather than chronologically organized, and some may have occurred during different phases of His Galilean ministry.

1. *Three Healings* (8:1-17)

These miracles have been understood by some to be a fulfillment of Isaiah 53:4. In these miracles Messiah uprooted the effects of sin (cf. 8:17).

a. Healing of a Leper (8:1-4)

Leprosy was believed to be a punishment for sin and the healing of leprosy a sign that Messiah was present (cf. Isa. 35:5-6; 61:1; Matt. 11:5). Whereas the Sermon on the Mount raised the listener's consciousness of sin, this miracle revealed the way of cleansing from sin. A leper was ceremonially unclean and not to be touched (Lev. 13:45; 22:4-6). Faith in the King's power and a willingness to heal (cf. 4:24) was coupled with honest humility. By touching the leper and yet remaining undefiled (2 Cor. 5:21), Jesus transcended the ceremonial law (Lev. 22:4-6) and operated by a higher principle (Matt. 22:37-40). When the cleansed leper reached the priests he could receive ceremonial cleansing (Lev. 14; Matt.

5:17) and the right to fellowship in Israel, and the priests would have a sign that Messiah had come. Silence about the miracle was necessary in Galilee so that Christ would not be hindered by a mass, superficial response (cf. Mark 1:45). If leprosy pictures sin, instant cleansing pictures instant forgiveness.

b. Healing of a Centurion's Servant (8:5-13)

Luke 7:1-10 records that Jewish elders representing the centurion came to Christ. When Christ conveyed that He would come, the centurion sent another messenger asking Him not to enter his house (and thereby defile Himself, John 18:28), but asking instead that Jesus heal his servant from a distance. The centurion understood the authority and mission of the King, and displayed both humility and faith (v. 8). Jesus was astonished at his attitude and used him to illustrate that many Gentiles would believe (cf. Isa. 2:2-3; 11:10) while many Jews would reject Him. The kingdom of heaven is described as a great feast (vv. 11-12; cf. Ps. 23:5; Rev. 19:9). "Sons of the kingdom" (v. 12) are Jews by birth only, unbelievers who rejected their spiritual heritage. They would be separated from the light of salvation to experience conscious eternal anguish. In contrast, faith in the Messiah transforms paralysis into life.

c. Healing of Peter's Mother-in-law (8:14-17)

Peter's mother-in-law may have been sick with malaria when the Lord touched her and restored her to instant health and vigor. It was on the Sabbath after a miracle at the synagogue (Mark 1:21-28). By evening, word had spread and many sick and demon-possessed people had been brought to the house. Matthew quotes Isaiah 53:4 to show how Christ fulfilled messianic expectations. "Took our infirmities, and carried away our diseases" (v. 17) can mean either He *carried* in the sense of bore the burden of, or *carried away,* that is, removed our diseases and infirmities. In this context Matthew means that He carried *the burden of* their infirmities and diseases. Christ fully felt the burden of the effects of sin. Every disease was ultimately a result of original sin and must have reminded Him of the cross He was to bear (Matt. 9:36; 14:14). Each healing miracle was an extension of His anticipated propitiation for sin (1 John 2:2), which He would accomplish on the cross (John 12:31-33). Full healing will come at the redemption of the body (Rom. 8:23).

2. *Implications of Discipleship* (8:18-22)

This account does not chronologically follow the three healings, but it is logically connected. Jesus told the inner circle of disciples that it was time to depart to the other side, apparently to obtain some respite from the growing crowds (v. 18). Just before departure two would-be disciples came forward. The first was an enthusiastic scribe whose commitment to follow Christ was built on a superficial understanding (vv. 19-20). The King and His followers would be pilgrims with their citizenship in heaven with no place on earth to call home. The term *Son of man,* although sometimes used of all men in their humanness (Ps. 8:4), is used as a special messianic title in Daniel 7:13 and throughout the gospels. When Christ formally claimed that title He was accused of blasphemy (Matt. 26:64-66). The second volunteer (vv. 21-22) was a disciple in the sense of a learner and not one who was fully committed. He wanted to become a member of the inner circle but would not be ready until he understood that spiritual family ties were deeper than physical family ties. Jesus was not condemning all attendance at unbelievers' funerals.

3. *Three Displays of Authority* (8:23—9:17)

After Jesus healed bodily disease in the first three miracles, He displayed power over nature and demons and the ability to forgive sin.

a. Authority over Nature (8:23-27)

Frequent sudden storms stirred the Sea of Galilee when cold air from Mount Hermon rushed down and clashed with the warm air at water level. This particular storm was so severe that it was called a great *shaking,* a great *seismos,* the word from which we get *seismograph.* Christ slept soundly at the stern of the boat (Mark 4:38), weary from His work. His rebuke of the disciples seems to indicate that they should have had sufficient appreciation of His presense not to be afraid of the storm. The miracle was twofold: immediately He both stopped the wind and calmed the sea. The disciples were startled at His power. Such control of the elements was a highly extolled attribute of Jehovah (Ps. 89:8-9). "What kind of man" (27) has the thought of *How wonderful a man is this!* (Luke 8:25). The King taught His subjects the value of His commitment to them. They would not die until their work was done (Job 5:26; Ps. 91).

b. Authority over Demons (8:28-34)

It was evening (cf. Mark 4:35; 5:1) when the boating party arrived at Kersa, or Karse, in the region of the larger city of Gadara of the Gadarenes. Two extremely dangerous demon-possessed men accosted the Lord and His disciples (v. 28). Mark and Luke confined their attention to the spokesman for the two (cf. Mark 5:2-6; Luke 8:27). The demons recognized the Messiah (v. 29), His authority (James 2:19), and their ultimate judgment (Rev. 20:2-3). They also knew they would be exorcised (cf. "since" [v. 31], not "if") and therefore, asked permission to enter the swine. The herdsmen observing the scene (vv. 30, 33) received clear evidence of Christ's supernatural power as the village's common herd of 2,000 pigs rushed to its death. The blind and calloused villagers came, not to rejoice and see their sick healed, but to beg Christ to leave (vv. 33-34). He did leave, but a new missionary remained in the region to witness for his new-found King (cf. Mark 5:18-20; Luke 8:38-39). Messiah taught at least two valuable lessons: He has authority over the dangerous spirit world that fights against His kingdom, and human lives are far more valuable than animals or possessions.

c. Authority over Sin (9:1-8)

Jesus recrossed the sea to His headquarters at Peter's house

in Capernaum, where a desperately ill paralytic was brought
to Him (cf. Mark 2:1-12). All misfortune is not *directly*
caused by sin (cf. John 9:3), but apparently this man's sin had
caused his misfortune, for Christ saw "their faith," and first
pronounced him forgiven, though not healed. And the paralytic took courage because his sins were forgiven, not because
he was healed (v. 2). The scribes correctly deduced that if
Christ were not God, He would be blaspheming (for only God
could ultimately forgive sin), but their conclusion was "evil"
(vv. 3-4), for Christ is God. The rhetorical question of verse 5
gives evidence that Jesus is the divine Messiah. Observers
could empirically test a claim to healing powers but not so
easily test a claim to spiritual authority. To heal or forgive required divine power. Logically, if Christ was able to do one,
He would be able to do the other. The paralytic again
responded in faith, and was immediately healed (v. 7). Many
were filled with awe over the feat (v. 8), but missed the point:
they glorified God for giving such authority to the human
race instead of recognizing that the title "Son of man" (v. 6)
and the act of forgiveness verified by the healing were ir-
refutable evidences that the divine Messiah was with them.

4. *Miracles Are Related to Feasting, Not Fasting* (9:9-17)

Between the second and third group of miracles Matthew
records his own recruitment to discipleship and his testi-
monial dinner (cf. Luke 5:27-29). The dinner raises two questions: (1) Why were publicans and sinners invited? and (2),
Why were they feasting instead of conducting the traditional
fast of humiliation as were John's disciples and the Pharisees? In answering those questions Matthew shows first that
the Messiah came to reach those sinners, and second, that His
presence and ministry called for joyful expressions such as
feasting rather than expressions of sorrow such as fasting.

As a publican in Capernaum, Matthew had probably been
witness to much of Christ's ministry. So when called (v. 9), he
readily forsook all to follow with his King (cf. Luke 5:28).
The Pharisees insinuated (v. 11) that Jesus showed Himself to
be a sinner by eating with publicans and sinners. In answer to

that accusation, the Lord declared that the purpose of a physician is to heal the sick; so His purpose as the spiritual physician was to heal the morally sick (v. 12). The Pharisees believed they were morally healthy, but if they truly had been righteous they would have, like the Physician, ministered to the sick. Christ instructed them to ponder Hosea 6:6 (cf. Matt. 12:7): religion without compassion is worthless, dead legalism (v. 13). His call is to repentance, to accept Him as Lord and Savior (cf. Luke 5:32).

The habitual, "man-made" fast of humiliation, discussed in verses 14-17 was going on during Matthew's feast (cf. Mark 2:18) and is logically and chronologically connected with this section. Such fasting was inappropriate for Christ's disciples. First, His public ministry was like a joyful wedding feast (cf. Isa. 62:5; Jer. 31:31-34), and groomsmen did not fast during the groom's wedding feast. After the Groom (Jesus) was rejected (i.e., crucified) fasting would be appropriate until His resurrection (cf. John 16:16-21). Second, this fasting would be like putting an unshrunk patch on a preshrunk garment or unfermented wine in a prestretched wineskin. A proper understanding of Messiah's presence would rip apart old traditions and burst asunder outmoded ways.

5. *Three Miracles of Restoration* (9:18-38)

Although four miracles are recorded here, the first, third, and fourth are most germane to Matthew's theme. A climax was reached in miracle one; miracle three established the legal testimony of two witnesses; and miracle four, an anticlimactic rejection of Christ, resulted in the antithesis of miracle one. Miracle two occurred on the same day as miracle one and was interwoven in the story of that day. Faith in Christ is a prominent element in each story. However, Matthew has already established that faith is not necessarily a prerequisite to a miracle (7:28-32; see also 11:20-24).

a. Restoration of Life (9:18-26)

While considering the question of fasting, Christ was interrupted by Jairus, a synogogue and community leader and a

pillar of orthodoxy (v. 18; cf. Mark 5:22-23; Luke 8:41-42).
Jairus demonstrated both humility and faith by bowing
before One his own community had rejected. Apparently he
twice requested that Jesus come, before and after his
daughter died (cf. Mark 5:22-43 and Luke 8:41-56). Augus-
tine suggests that Matthew brings together both requests in
verse 18. Jesus immediately responded and with Peter, James,
and John (cf. Mark 5:37) started toward Jairus's home
(v. 19).

On their way, a significant parenthesis took place in the
story. They passed a severely ill woman who took advantage
of the opportunity to be healed (v. 20-22). Her hemorrhage
was humanly incurable (Luke 8:44) bringing her physical and
emotional weakness. As a result, she was considered a social
outcast and ceremonially unclean (Lev. 15:25). As Jesus
passed she "came up behind Him and touched the fringe of
His cloak" (v. 20). At once she "was made well" (v. 21). This
was not a psychosomatic healing; Jesus literally perceived

power coming out of Him (Mark 5:30). He turned and publicly rewarded the woman's faith.

Verses 23-26 finish the story of Jairus's daughter. The
mourners in the house were paid professionals, capable of a
good act. When Jesus stated that the girl was asleep, the
psuedo-mourners "laughed Him down" and were ejected for
their unbelief. Jesus did not literally mean that the girl was
asleep, but that her death was not permanent (cf. John
11:11-15). Matthew records that Christ raised the dead (11:5),
but this is the only account he relates that possibly could fit
such an event. With this climactic miracle (cf. v. 26), Christ's
ministry reached a zenith.

b. Restoration of Sight (9:27-31)

This sign, found only in Matthew, logically follows the
restoration to life. Resuscitation is a picture of salvation
(13:16; 15:14), and with salvation comes new spiritual sight:
hence, the healing of two blind men. "Son of David" (v. 27)
was a popular messianic title in New Testament times (cf.

Matt. 21:15-16). The blind men evidenced both faith and respect. Christ knew their hearts, but questioned them to encourage a public confession (v. 28). Every legal testimony was to be established by two witnesses (cf. Deut. 19:15; Matt. 8:28; 20:30-34). Again, *faith* and a *touch* resulted in healing (v. 30). To protect His ministry from thrill-seekers, Christ once more charged the healed men to remain silent.

c. Restoration of Speech (9:32-34)

This miracle, which is unique to Matthew's account, was coupled with the previous sign as fulfillment of Isaiah 35:5-6. The powerful spirit being that indwelt that man prevented him from talking. When Christ cast out the demon and enabled the man to speak the people were amazed (v. 33), but the Pharisees willfully rejected the truth (v. 34). Because the Pharisees could not deny that supernatural power was at work and did not want to be convicted of sin, they attributed His power to Satan. Such rejection of God's testimony that Jesus Christ is Lord closed the door to the kingdom of heaven (Matt. 12:24-32). This was the first of several anticlimactic reactions to Christ that grew to murderous intensity (cf. Matt. 10:25).

The section from 8:1—9:38 is summarized in verse 35 with what is almost a repeat of Matthew 4:23. Matthew 9:36-38 emphasizes the effect of the Galilean campaign on Christ: "He felt compassion" (v. 36; i.e., He suffered with those in distress). The sheep-shepherd metaphor was a familiar one to the Jews. As Christ saw those forlorn suffering "sheep" coming to Him, His heart went out to them and He instructed His disciples to pray for "harvesters" (vv. 37-38), people who would be sent by God to minister to those with spiritual, emotional, or physical hurt.

4

THE KING'S MESSENGERS

C. MESSENGERS OF THE KING (10:1-42)

The twelve specially picked disciples (i.e., *learners*) were elevated to the position of apostles (cf. Luke 6:12-13, 20; i.e., *sent ones*) and in the process became the answer to their own prayer for *harvesters* (cf. 9:35-38). In preparing His apostles for their first mission, Jesus delivered His second sermon recorded in Matthew. That this is one sermon rather than a collection of Jesus' sayings is made clear by his introduction (10:5) and conclusion (11:1). Most of the ideas found in this address are repeated in other circumstances (cf. chaps. 24-25; Luke 10:4-12; 21:16). Only verses 5-8 and 40-42 with their messianic implications are unique to Matthew. Christ here extended His own messianic authority as Prophet, Priest, and King. His wonderful words and works would be duplicated by His apostles. Note the careful distinction between casting out spirits and healing diseases (v. 1). There is an orderly development in this address, similar to that of the Sermon on the Mount. In verses 2-4 the twelve apostles are named; given a charge in verses 5-15; prepared for the inevitable persecution (vv. 16-23); given an antidote to resultant fear (vv. 24-33); given an admonition to keep the Lord first (vv. 34-39); and provided with a concluding encouragement about rewards (vv. 40-42).

1. *The Twelve Apostles* (10:2-4)

Names of the twelve apostles are arranged in three groups of four. By comparing the biographical data in each of the four listings in the New Testament (cf. 10:2-4; Mark 3:16-19; Luke 6:14-16; Acts 1:13, 26), we can determine that James the son of Alphaeus is James the Less; Bartholomew is probably Nathanael; and Thaddaeus is Judas the son of James in Luke, and not Judas "Iscariot" in John. Each group begins with the same name with Peter occupying the place of preeminence. Only in this gospel is Matthew called the *publican,* possibly intimating that he wrote this gospel. Those men of moderate ability had contrasting personalities; note the optimism of Peter (14:28; 26:33, 35) and the pessimism of Thomas (John 11:16; 20:24-25); Thaddaeus was a zealot dedicated to the overthrow of Rome and Matthew had been a tax collector for the government. The listing in pairs may correspond to the pairs sent out two by two (Mark 6:7).

2. *The Charge to The Twelve* (10:5-15)

The apostles' exclusive mission was to announce the arrival of the kingdom of heaven to the Jews. Matthew alone records that fact in verses 5-8. After the crucifixion and resurrection of the Messiah, the Jewish probation would be over and the gospel would then go out to the whole world (cf. Matt. 28:19; Acts 1:8). Instructions in verses 9-10 were temporary (cf. Luke 22:35-36). Two reasons for not taking extra provisions can be assumed: They had confidence in their King to provide (cf. 6:19-34), and they were worthy of support (cf. 1 Cor. 9:7, 14; 1 Tim. 5:18). The few available inns made hospitality a necessary quality of Christian character (1 Tim. 3:2). So as not to be needlessly encumbered, they were to stay only where received and to take only what was necessary. A walking stick was not to be taken unless appropriate (cf. v. 10 and Mark 6:8). The greeting of *peace* (v. 12) literally resulted in the peace of God residing within certain families (cf. Num. 6:24-26; John 20:19). Shaking dust off their feet was a familiar Jewish custom that prevented heathen soil from being transported back to the Holy Land. By applying that custom to unbelieving Jews, Christ showed that such Israelites were really pagans (cf. Acts 13:50-51). Refusal to accept the offer to enter Christ's kingdom would bring disastrous results (vv. 14-15; Gen. 13:13; Luke 12:47-48; Jude 7).

3. *Preparation for Persecution* (10:16-23)

This first journey was to be relatively peaceful (cf. Luke 22:35), but hostility would dramatically increase. Synagogues or local sanhedrins (v. 17) were to become the sites of formal persecution. Gentile governors and Jewish kings would hear Holy Spirit-empowered testimony, (vv. 19:20; cf. Matt. 27:26; Acts 4:13; 12:1; 25:13, 24, 26; 1 Pet. 3:15ff). Faithfulness to the will of God even divides families (v. 21, cf. Mic. 7:6; Matt. 5:10-16; 10:24; Mark 3:21; John 7:5). But the faithful would endure all persecution and ultimately be delivered (v. 22). Further light on this relatively obscure period of exclusive ministry to the Jews is found in Matthew 24:9-14 and Galatians 2:7-9. Such missionary activities would not be completed before the glorious second coming of their King (v. 23; cf. Matt. 16:27-28; 19:28; 24:27, 30, 37, 39, 44; 25:31; 26:64). That glorious coming would be foreshadowed by His resurrection from the grave (John 20:19-29) and the prophesied fall of Jerusalem in A.D. 70 (cf. Matt. 22:7; 23:38; 24:2, 15-21).

4. *Antidote for Fear* (10:24-33)

The Jews would call Christ *Beelzebub* (v. 25, cf. 2 Kings 1:2-3, 6; Matt. 8:34; 12:26-27). The apostles could expect similar accusations. Because it would be their distinction to suffer as did their Lord, Christ gave them three reasons they should not fear: first, nothing is hidden from their God (v. 26); second, God will protect their immortal being (soul), which cannot be destroyed by men (v. 28); and, third, their God has a deep concern for the lesser elements of His creation and therefore can be expected to have a much greater concern for their lives (vv. 29-31). The verb tense of verse 33 refers to a continual life of rejection as contrasted by Peter's momentary denial.

5. *Keep Messiah First* (10:34-39)

Although Messiah came to bring peace He sometimes brought the *sword,* for judgment must precede peace (v. 34). Christ emphasized one aspect of the truth (i.e., judgment) to cause His listeners to stop short and think. Matthew is the gospel of rejection. Verses 35-37 can be taken as another allusion to Micah 7:6 (cf. Matt. 10:21). To take up one's *cross* is to follow God's will for one's life and thereby be willing to suffer for Christ and die even as He did (16:24). Verse 38, a prophetic allusion to His death, is the first mention of a cross in Matthew. The person's life is equated to the person himself (v. 39; cf. Luke 9:23-24).

6. *Encouragement of a Prophet's Reward* (10:40-42)

To receive and encourage a prophet of God one must have the same heart as a prophet and be worthy of the same reward. Those who would receive the Master's envoy would be receiving the Master Himself (cf. 1 Kings, 17:8-16; 2 Kings 4:8-37). Christ ended His second sermon on that encouraging note.

5

THE KING'S OPPOSITION

D. OPPOSITION TO THE KING (11:1—12:50)

Opposition to Messiah increased. John was imprisoned, the religious leaders and their followers refused to repent, superficial Sabbath controversies clouded the true issue, and the unpardonable sin was committed by some. Through it all Christ remained true to His mission.

1. *Encouragement and Praise for the Forerunner* (11:1-19)

Messiah's gracious words and works (v. 1) precipitated a question from John the Baptist (vv. 2-3). After his arrest by Herod Antipas of Galilee, the Baptist was imprisoned in a section of the fortress of Machaerus, located near the Dead Sea. He was allowed visitors, but information concerning Christ was fragmentary. John had preached that those who rejected Messiah would be baptized with fire (Matt. 3:7, 10). But instead of judgment, John heard of mercy and grace being extended to sinners. Having confused the first and second comings of Messiah, John could not understand why Christ, if He was truly the Messiah, was not forcibly and openly asserting His messianic claims. Why too, was he himself left in prison? Messiah's answer (vv. 4-6) was sufficient to reassure John. Christ described His works by utilizing the phraseology of Old Testament prophecy (cf. Isa. 35:5-10; 61:1), thereby reaffirming that indeed He was the Messiah.

John is not to be disparaged for his honest doubt (vv. 7-15). Christ praised His forerunner as a man of both strong conviction and absolute dedication, who turned from the comforts of soft living to a spartan existence to best complete his mission (v. 8). John was more significant than any Old Testament prophet (v. 9). His ministry was prophesied (cf. Mal. 3:1), and he not only announced the coming of Messiah but was there to point Him out when He arrived. Although the Baptist was not literally Elijah (cf. John 1:21), his attitude was similar to that of Elijah (Matt. 17:12). Because John would die before experiencing first-hand the greatest benefits of the kingdom of heaven, those who in their earthly lives did experience the kingdom blessings would receive a greater privilege than even John (v. 11; cf. 13:16-17). The *violence* that the kingdom of heaven *suffers* (v. 12) probably refers to the persecution of Christ and His disciples. However, those who enter the kingdom do face a great struggle against spiritual forces. Christ's admonition in verse 15 is one of the most repeated exhortations in all of His preaching and teaching: "He who has ears to hear, let him hear." Listen and *respond*—that's what ears are for!

The rejection of Christ and His forerunner by that "generation" is illustrated in the parable of the children playing in the market place (vv. 16-19). One group of children chided the other for being discontent and not playing with them no matter what game was suggested. Because children tire easily, are restless, and always want to start something new, their natural self-centeredness often brings games to a quarrelsome end. Those childish attitudes describe that generation of unbelievers. They rejected John ostensibly because he was too austere, solemn, and ascetic. They rejected Christ because He was too joyful and free and even ate with publicans and sinners. The members of that generation could not be pleased. They actually rejected John because he called them to repentance, and Christ because the kindgom He offered was not to their liking. That same message was presented by both John and Jesus; therefore, to reject the Messiah's messenger was in effect to reject the Messiah. The wisdom of the variant life-styles of John and Jesus was vindicated by the changed lives of their disciples. Those changed lives were the *deeds* of verse 19.

2. *Cursing or Reward for that Generation* (11:20-30)

The theme of rejection is further illustrated in the careless, indifferent attitude of the greatly privileged Galilean cities (vv. 20:25). "Then" (v. 20) refers to a middle or later point in Christ's Galilean ministry. Ancient cities such as Tyre and Sidon were judged for their materialistic, proud, and cruel attitudes (Isa. 23; Ezek. 26—28); and Sodom and Gomorrah, for their injustice, idolatry, and sexual sins. But the ultimate judgment of the people of the Galilean cities would be far more severe than the judgment those ancient cities had faced. Bethsaida was Philip's home and the place from where Andrew and Peter originally came (John 1:44). Chorazin had also received extended ministry. Capernaum was the seat of Christ's headquarters during His Galilean campaign (Matt. 4:13). "The day of judgment" is that final great white throne judgment (Rev. 20:11-15). Rejection of Christ would bring a worse eternal judgment upon those who had received the greatest light and yet rejected the gracious offer. "Hades" here is hell, the place of eternal torments and fire (Luke 16:23-24).

Christ rejoices, not in condemnation, but in rewarding those who do respond to Him (vv. 25-30). This passage is recorded only in Matthew. "At that time," (v. 25) was after the early days of popularity and when opposition was growing. The seventy disciples had recently returned with their report of some conversions (cf. Luke 10:1, 17, 21-22). Christ praised the Father for His will (vv. 25-26) and displayed a most unique familiarity and intimate relationship with Him as the Son (v. 27), reminiscent of the emphasis in John's gospel (cf. John 10:30). "These things" (v. 25) refers to the plan of salvation, and the "wise and intelligent" are those who think their sound human reasoning without divine revelation will lead them to salvation. The contrast is between those who trust their earthly wisdom to save them and those who do not. Although it was primarily the uneducated who turned to Christ, a highly educated person could be a "babe" who was drawn to Christ and an unlearned person could be the wise and intelligent who blindly rejected Him. Ignorance is neither an advantage nor a disadvantage. The "all things" (v. 27) includes authority over Satan, his demons, nature, life, and death (cf. chaps. 1—11; 28:18). "Come to Me" (v. 28) means to believe in Christ. The "heavy-laden" are described in Matthew 23:4 as those who are overburdened with the law and its attendant interpretations. Christ's offer for men to put their lives together under His direction (i.e., receive *peace*) does not suggest a freedom from toil, but deliverance from guilt, futility, and crushing anxiety. A *yoke* enabled a burden to be evenly distributed on a carrier and was metaphorically used by the rabbis to speak of the total obligations a person was expected to take upon himself. To take Christ's yoke is to become one of His disciples. Contrast the alternative in Acts 15:10. Christ gives rest (v. 28) and His disciples find it (v. 29). Men can only receive what Christ has given.

3. *Sabbath Controversies* (12:1-21)

This is our Lord's final break with the synogogue. It arose out of His reinterpretation of the Sabbath law. The fourth commandment, to "not do any work" on the Sabbath day (Ex. 20:8-10; Deut. 5:14), led the rabbis to stipulate thirty-nine different activities that constituted *work*. Reaping, threshing, and winnowing grain as well as preparing a meal were among the traditional prohibitions. Their misinterpretation of the law (v. 2) was corrected by Christ (vv. 3-8). Messiah vindicated His disciples on the basis of four arguments recorded by Matthew: (1) If David was not wrong when necessity led him to break a ceremonial law, eat the showbread of the Tabernacle, and share it with his followers (1 Sam. 21:1-6), then David's great grandson, Jesus, was not wrong to allow His disciples to break a *tradition* about the Sabbath when necessity so dictated. Human needs take precedence over ritual service (vv. 3, 14); (2) If the priests violated the Pharasaic definition of work by offering extra sacrifices and performing other necessary functions (Lev. 24:8; Num. 28:8ff) and yet were blameless, they must have operated by a

higher law than the Pharasaic interpretation. Therefore, the
Sabbath law as they interpreted it was not inviolate. The
priests were serving the Temple that was believed to enshrine
the divine presence. But Jesus stood before them as God in-
carnate and, therefore, represented something greater than
the Temple. If the Sabbath law could be broken for the lesser,
it could be broken for the greater (vv. 5-6; cf. Matt.
12:41-42). (3) The laws of God in general and the Sabbath law
in particular were designed to be of benefit to man, not a
burden (Mark 2:27). No law is truly fulfilled when its spirit
and most basic purpose is impinged. Hosea 6:6, here quoted,
stresses that mercy is more important than ritual. The absence
of mercy can not be overcome by the offering of sacrifices,
however numerous. If the Pharisees had correctly understood
the law, they would not have condemned Christ's disciples.
To honor life by being compassionate is more important to
Messiah than to keep a tradition that violates life (vv. 7, 11);
(4) Christ added a climactic point in verse 8: the Son of Man is
sovereign over all laws. Here Christ claimed His deity: "For"
in picking the grain His disciples were recognizing His lordship rather than the lordship of the Pharisees and their tradition. His disciples were right in doing that, for Christ is the
"Lord of the Sabbath." How could one honor the Sabbath
while dishonoring the Lord of the Sabbath? We have a
moment-by-moment Sabbath (Heb. 4:8-9, 14).

The second Sabbath controversy (vv. 9-14) was encouraged
by the Pharisees that they might have legal recourse against
Christ (v. 10). Their attitude showed how far they had drifted
from an understanding of the character of Jehovah. They
allowed an act of healing on the Sabbath only if it was
necessary to preserve life. Christ's carefully chosen question
(v. 11) exposed their callous unconcern. His contention was
that healing on the Sabbath was most appropriate because it
honored the true meaning of the Sabbath—the alleviation of
burdens. He was angered at their cold legalism (Mark 3:5).
Because Pharasaic tradition allowed one to pull his animal
from a pit on the Sabbath, and because man is of more value

than an animal, it was lawful by their precedent to pull a sick man from his "pit" (i.e., affliction) on the Sabbath. Mercy is always right (Mic. 6:6-8). When the man with the withered hand responded positively to Christ's concern, he was immediately healed (v. 13). The irony of the negative response of the Pharisees (v. 14) is that they thought it wrong to heal on the Sabbath, but not wrong to plot murder. Matthew takes us one step closer to the cross (cf. 10:38).

Full awareness of the murder plot (v. 15) did not deter Christ from His mission. His stability amidst the worst provocation exemplified the depth of His graciousness and gentleness (v. 20). Those who needed help and knew it left the synagogue and followed Him and were healed (v. 15). Apparently that was the breaking point between Jesus and the synagogue community. The reappearance of the secrecy motif (cf. Matt. 8:4; 9:30; 12:16) does help to explain why Christ was not more widely known then, but was primarily included by Matthew for the purpose of showing how Christ fulfilled the predicted picture of the Messiah (vv. 18:21; cf. Isa. 42:1-4). Messiah did not call undue attention to Himself in the performance of His mission (v. 19). The post-resurrection ministry among Gentiles is in verse 21 (cf. Matt. 28:19). Messiah did not despise the weak, but He Himself was not weak. He neither failed nor was He discouraged, and He will one day see justice established on the earth.

4. *The One Unpardonable Sin* (12:22-37)

Rejection of the Holy Spirit's testimony that Jesus Christ is the Son of God is unpardonable. This blasphemous climax (v. 24) explains the attitude that resulted in Christ's crucifixion. Matthew relates the setting (vv. 22-24), establishes Christ's justification of His power (vv. 25-30), and records Messiah's irrevocable condemnation of those who reject the Spirit's testimony about Him (vv. 31-37).

As a result of a spectacular exorcism (v. 22) the multitude raised the question that Jesus might be the "Son of David," the Messiah. By contrast, the Pharisees suggested that Satan,

"Beelzebub" (the ruler of demons), gave Jesus authority over demons (v. 24).

Christ refuted the Pharasaic accusation on three grounds: (1) If Satan had given Him the authority to curtail demonic activity, He would be defeating Himself. Civil war is always self-destructive (vv. 25-26); (2) the Pharisees and their pupils (i.e., "sons"; v. 27) claimed success in exorcism. If Christ used Satan's power in this activity, the Pharisees and their disciples could be accused of the same thing. Before His third argument, Christ offered another explanation: His ministry was performed by the Spirit of God and, therefore, the kingdom of God had come (v. 28); (3) for Satan ("the strong man," v. 29) to be hindered, he would have to meet one with superior power who could bind him. Christ is that superior power who has authority over Satan (cf. 4:1-11; 11:27). This binding was evidenced in the wilderness temptations and in the healing, forgiving, and restoring ministries of Christ from the outset of His public ministry. Satan's power over the lives of men was broken (vv. 28-29) but not completely impotent. Jesus took furniture from Satan's house (Israel) as the souls of men were set free.

Condemnation of all who assumed the Pharasaic attitude is stressed in verses 30-37. The campaign between Satan and God was raging and neutrality was impossible. Eventually, all mankind will be divided into two camps—those who accept the Spirit's testimony and those who reject it (v. 30). As Christ was gathering out of Satan's house, the Pharisees were scattering those that Christ would gather. Because rejection of the Spirit's testimony leaves man to his own human reasoning (cf. 11:25-27), he cannot know the way of salvation and, therefore, cannot be forgiven (vv. 31-32). The hypocrisy of those religious leaders who committed the unpardonable sin is seen in their claim to be good healthy fruit trees. In reality they were producing rotten fruit (vv. 33-37). Christ challenged them to be honest, to declare their rottenness (making the "tree bad"), or repent (make the "tree good") so that the fruit will also be good (v. 33). By accusing Christ of being an extension of Satan's kingdom they disclosed that at heart they were really like a "brood of vipers" (v. 34). Christ warned of a careless attitude toward His Spirit-empowered testimony (vv. 36-37; cf. Matt. 11:23-24). A *careless* word is a useless and ineffective word. What earlier had a curse pronounced on it (cf. Isa. 5:20) here is called *blasphemy* against the Holy Spirit. This blasphemy is a calculated, knowledgeable, and permanent rejection of Christ. It is not a sin of reason; it is a sin of the heart, the essence of being. When the Pharisees could no longer ignore or deny Christ's testimony, they rejected it.

5. *The Sign of Jonah* (12:38-45)

Matthew includes this account to show how the religious leaders kept asking for further proof of Christ's Person, although sufficient evidence already had been offered (11:16-19). The sign they requested (v. 38) must have been something different from the miracles that previously had been performed by Christ, which the leaders explained away as demonic. Possibly they wanted a sign similar to one He refused to give when He was tempted in the wilderness (4:5-7). Such a sign would have left no room for faith. For the leaders to ask for another sign after all that Christ had done was to expose their impudent, hypocritical, and insulting spiritual blindness. Christ condemned them as an "evil and adulterous generation" (v. 39) that would receive only the sign of Jonah (vv. 39-40). That sign (His resurrection) would grow out of the necessity for Christ to complete His mission (16:21), not out of a need to provide more evidence to the unbelieving community. The three days and three nights Jonah "spent in the belly of the sea monster" (v. 40) are idiomatic for a block of time and may not refer to seventy-two literal hours. To prove their condemnation Christ compared their circumstances with two previous generations. Neither "Nineveh" (v. 41) nor the "Queen of the South" (cf. v. 42; 1 Kings 10:13) had received the clarity of testimony that the Pharisees had received. Yet, they repented and would stand as a testimony against the Pharisees at the final judgment. Christ as the Son of God is greater than Jonah and Solomon just as the architect is greater than the building he creates (Heb. 3:3).

The short parable in verses 43-45 equates Israel to a man whose life (house) is exorcised of demons but who remains unrepentant and, therefore, faces greater condemnation. Christ was exorcising demons from Israel, but unrepentance left Israel empty of God and open to greater demonic attack and ultimately greater condemnation at the last judgment.

6

THE KING'S PARABLES

E. PARABLES OF THE KING (13:1-58)

In this third discourse Matthew records seven parables apparently delivered after Christ's break with the synagogue establishment and the blasphemous accusation of the Pharisees that His power was from Satan (cf. chaps. 11—12). There were at least two reasons for His speaking to the unbelieving multitudes in parables: by hiding the meaning of the parable He (1) brought a prophesied judgment against the willfully blind, and (2) protected Himself from further hostility from the unbelieving crowd. When interpreted, however, the parable that had become a riddle to the unreceptive heart gave His disciples a clearer understanding of the truth.

Typically, Matthew uses a mass of material on a subject to heighten the effect of his point (cf. the deity of Christ stressed by miracles in 8:1—9:38). This group of parables emphasizes a cataclysmic change in Christ's public teaching: from His open declaration of the truth to the unbelieving multitudes to withholding such truth from the unreceptive heart. The teaching technique previously used to illustrate and confirm an obvious truth now conveyed riddles that needed to be privately interpreted to His followers.

These parables unravel a *mystery,* something not revealed in the Old Testament but made known in the New (cf. Col. 1:26). Here the mystery pertains to one aspect of the kingdom of heaven, that is, the life of God in the hearts of disciples between the first and second comings of Messiah. Christ spoke the first four parables from an off-shore boat on the Sea of Galilee to a fascinated, unbelieving multitude on shore

(vv. 1-2). These parables, found only in Matthew, stress the eternal growth of the kingdom of heaven. The last three, along with the interpretation of the sower and tares parables, were spoken privately in a house to the disciples and stressed the internal nature of the kingdom.

1. *Parable of the Sower* (13:3-23)

Jesus explained why some accepted and many rejected His ministry. The effect of the seed is dependent on the state of the soil, not on the Sower or the seed. The seed is always good and life-giving. In Palestine when seed was sown by hand it was indiscriminately cast in all directions before plowing. Four kinds of soil are described and all are found in the same field (vv. 3-9). No impression could be made on the wayside soil, which was a well-trodden pathway along or through the field. Birds quickly devoured the exposed seed. The rocky soil, prevalent in Palestine, was covered by a thin layer of fertile earth. The underlying rock made the earth warm and seed quickly germinated. But without sufficient roots the new shoots withered in the sun. Thorny soil also gave an intimation of fruitfulness, but produced thistles that choked out the shoots of the good seed.

Up to this point Christ's teaching had been clear; here the meaning of the parable was hidden. So His disciples asked Him why He spoke to the multitude in ambiguous terms (v. 10). Christ answered their question (vv. 11-17) and interpreted the parable for them (vv. 18-23). Although Matthew interjects that scene here, it occurred later in the house (cf. Mark 4:10). Christ's answer has two basic points. First, divine mysteries cannot be understood without divine help (cf. John 3:3), and divine help is a matter of pure grace (Dan. 4:24; 1 Cor. 4:7). That undeserved help was not given to members of the multitude (v. 11). They would either progress or regress, but not stand still. Any who progressed would know the blessing of God as a guarantee of future *abundant* blessing; the regressor was guaranteed further deprivation (v. 12). It was because of the willful spiritual regression of the unbelieving multitude that Christ spoke in parables (v. 13). Liberal critics are unwilling to believe that Christ could have adopted that policy. But the principle is proved even in the natural realm: unused abilities atrophy. Second, Christ's use of parables or *riddles,* as the Aramaic word may be translated, further demonstrated God's principles of judgment pronounced on the Israelites of Isaiah's day (cf. v. 14; Isa. 6:9). Both in Isaiah's day and during Christ's ministry, the people decided neither to see nor hear the Word of God, and God decided to punish them by allowing them to have their way (cf. Prov. 29:1 and Pharaoh's life, Ex. 7:22; 8:15, 19, 32; 9:7). Again Christ placed heavy stress on human responsibility: "Seeing they do not see, and hearing they do not hear." Having anesthetized their hearts to Christ's words and works, the people would then reap the result. In contrast, the disciples were *blessed;* God's favor was resting on them. Many faithful Old Testament saints who yearned for such a privilege died in faith, not seeing their hope fulfilled (cf. Isa. 64:1: Heb. 11:13, 40).

In His interpretation of the parable (vv. 18-23) Christ revealed that the seed is the Word of God, the message from the King about His kingdom (v. 19, cf. Luke 8:11). The sower is the Son of Man (v. 37) and by extension all who represent Him (cf. 10:40). The ground is the human heart (i.e., *anyone,* v. 19*a*). Unresponsive, self-hardened hearts are symbolized by the *wayside* soil from which the good seed of the Word is snatched by the devil before it can germinate. Such were the Pharisees, scribes, and their followers. Only if God plows the heart with trouble is there hope the seed will take root. *Rocky places* (vv. 19-20) represent those who superficially make an emotional but untrue response to the gospel (cf. 8:19-20; 26:24, doom; 27:3 and Judas's emotional repentance). The impulsive person is easily touched but does not allow the seed to take root. When things do not work out as planned, he realizes that he has not counted the cost and is let down. The word literally means trapped or snared. Such a person is ensnared by his disappointment and falls away. Irreconcilable loyalties describe the (*thorny soil*)(v. 22). This heart is easily preoccupied with lesser concerns. For the rich man it may be his luxuries (cf. 19:16-22); for the poor man his financial obligation. The *cares* are weeds that choke out the Word and prevent the anticipated harvest (cf. Eph. 4:14). The fact that some seed was sown in good soil, responsive hearts, makes up for all the unproductive sowing. Abundant production from the (good soil serves) as an encouragement to all who sow the Word in the hearts of would-be disciples (v. 23). Thus, the effect the Word has is determined by the character of the hearer.

2. *Parable of the Tares* (13:24-30)

Whereas the last parable spoke of unproductive soil, this one speaks of bad seed. The kingdom of heaven resembles the situation of a good farmer who has sown his field with seed and then gone to rest. An enemy invades the field at night and attempts to ruin his crop by sowing *tares,* a species of rye grass that is host to a fungus that, if eaten by men or animals, is poisonous. In early stages, tares resemble wheat but are easily distinguishable as maturity is reached. In the parable, when farm hands observed an inordinate number of tares growing among the wheat, they would ask to weed the field. But the farmer, realizing that the intertwined root systems would make it impossible to pull up the tares without also uprooting some of the wheat, advised waiting until harvest time. Then the field could be completely harvested and the wheat stored in the barn. The tares, clearly discernable, could be separated into bundles to be burned. The kingdom of heaven resembles the farmer's situation in that it too has bad grain in its midst and must await the *harvest* before the good and bad are separated. Matthew records Christ's interpretation of the parable in verses 36-43.

3. *The Mustard Seed and Leaven* (13:31-35)

Although these two parables are not explained, they probably refer to the effects of the gospel preached during this age, as do the two previous parables.

The mustard seed is the smallest garden seed. Here it is often interpreted as depicting the seeming limited effect of the gospel during Jesus' time and the assurance that it would grow into a worldwide, observable influence. The Old Testament also teaches that spiritually great results develop from small beginnings. "Birds of the air" (v. 32) may refer to Gentiles who come to the gospel, which is rooted in Judaism (cf. Dan. 4:7, 12, 21).

The leaven depicts the silent, unobserved, yet permeating power of the gospel, which ultimately effects change in men and their culture. Not until the return of Christ as King of kings and Lord of lords (Rev. 19:16) will the world entirely be set straight (cf. Isa. 21:9). Until then disciples are to bring every thought into submission and harmony with the mind and will of Christ (2 Cor. 10:5) that every domain of life might exalt Him. These two parables thus teach that disciples are to have patience, exercise faith, and keep on praying and working. God's program cannot fail.

In verses 34-35 Matthew states that He sees Christ's use of parables as a fulfillment of Psalm 78:2, where *parables* are used in equivalence to *riddles*. Jesus used parables to reveal truth to believers and yet conceal truth from unbelievers (cf. 13:11). Jesus was the antitype of Asaph, the prophet-poet who wrote Psalm 78.

4. *Explanation of the Parable of the Tares* (13:36-43)

When He was alone with His disciples in the home of a friend (cf. Matt. 9:38; 12:46; 13:1) Jesus responded to a request to interpret the parable of the tares (cf. 13:51; Mark 4:34). John's ministry seemed to indicate an imminent judgment of unbelievers by God, the ax "already laid at the root" (Matt. 3:10-12). This parable seems to contradict that thought. The key concept of the parable is that the disciples must have patience until the fruit ripens for the delayed final judgment. The great consummation of the kingdom had begun and was literally *at hand* (Matt. 4:17). The humble seed sower was the "Son of Man" of Daniel 7:13 who would be given dominion, glory, and royal power. The field is the world and includes all aspects of culture that are to be influenced by the gospel.

Good seed are those in whom the kingdom message of salvation through repentance and faith has borne fruit. The *tares* are the sons of the evil one, Satan's followers, those in whom Satan's lies and half-truths produce a harvest of corruption.

At the end of the age, angels under the jurisdiction of the Lord will harvest the crop (cf. Matt. 24:31; Rev. 14:17-20). Those who rejected the grace of God will experience unquenchable, everlasting fire (cf. Dan. 12:2). Their bonds never end (Jude 6-7; cf. Rev. 14:9-11; 19:3; 20:10). Those who trust Christ have *everlasting life,* and those who reject Him suffer *everlasting punishment* (Matt. 25:46). The day of judgment represents the ultimate cleansing of the kingdom (vv. 40-42). Christ's and the Father's glory is partially reflected among believers now (2 Cor. 3:18) and someday will be fully reflected (v. 43; 1 John 3:23; Rev. 3:12). He who "has ears" must make a twofold examination: (1) to see whether he is best represented by the wheat or the tares; and (2) to determine if he is impatient for the fulfillment of the will of God. Christ rebuked His disciples for impetuous action (Luke 9:49-50). If the last judgment were left to men, wheat as well as weeds would probably be uprooted. Universal righteousness and peace cannot be expected until the King comes to establish His kingdom fully; "Then will the righteous shine forth as the sun" (v. 43).

5. The Parables of the Hidden Treasure: the Pearl of Great Price, and the Dragnet (13:44-50)

The remainder of the parables in this group apparently were spoken privately to the disciples. The hidden treasure and valuable pearl teach the inestimable value of salvation offered by the Messiah. The value is so great that at any price (even one's life) it would be a gift. Salvation is the supreme treasure. The worker surprised by the unexpected discovery of a great hidden treasure (v. 44) may be personified in Paul's experience (Acts 9:1-19) and others who unexpectedly met Christ (cf. John 4:1-44; 9:1-12). Some diligently search for the meaning and purpose of life as exemplified by the man who finds the most valuable pearl (v. 45; cf. Acts 8:26-38; 10:1-8, 30-33; 16:14; 17:10-12). In both parables the discoverers immediately recognize the great value of their *find* and are willing to surrender everything to possess it. Money will not buy salvation; it is God's free gift (Isa. 55:1). God has already paid the supreme price (John 3:16). Man can only gratefully and thankfully receive God's love gift (John 1:12; Eph. 2:18). These parables stress the *value* of salvation, not the *means* of salvation.

The parable of the dragnet (vv. 47-49) resembles the parable of the tares. Although the imagery is unique the lesson is the same: be patient, judgment is coming. A reiteration of verse 42 is found in verse 50. When the Lord repeated a point, it was for special emphasis. What clearer way to emphasize the reality of the final judgment than with a picture that disciples were very familiar with—the separation of good and bad fish from a dragnet. They would carry that poignant reminder into their future ministries.

6. *Understanding Parabolic Truth* (13:51-52)

It is doubtful the disciples understood all that Christ had spoken to them in parables, but they had a clearer idea of the mysteries of God's grace and judgment in the kingdom of heaven. A disciple of Christ is likened to the head of a household who has the responsibility to provide for the members of the house from his *old* and *new* treasures. The old treasure refers to that which was found in the Old Testament and the new treasure refers to Christ's further revelation concerning the timeless truths of the kingdom of heaven. The old truths are to be proclaimed in new forms and new relationships. The gospel, always the same, is to be uniquely applied to every age.

7. *Rejection of Christ at Nazareth* (13:53-58)

Christ's rejection at Nazareth is aptly recorded here on the heels of His parabolic teaching, for it is partially because of rejection that He used parables. According to Mark 6:2 these events transpired on the Sabbath day. The depth of the wisdom of Christ's teaching astonished the people, but their pettiness and probable envy prevented them from humbling themselves to the truth. Instead of trusting Him as their Messiah they used His humble origin as an excuse to be repelled by Him. The unbelief of His brothers was, however, ultimately turned to faith (cf. John 7:5; Acts 1:14). In verse 57 Christ claimed to be a prophet (cf. Deut. 18:15, 18; Matt. 21:11; Acts 3:22). Although some may have been healed by Christ in spite of imperfect faith, God-given faith is obviously a tremendous impetus, and unbelief a terrible hindrance. Many did not come to Christ for healing because they did not believe in Him (v. 58). Christ then withdrew and began to focus on the faithful.

7

THE KING'S WITHDRAWAL

F. WITHDRAWAL OF THE KING (14:1—16:12)

Rejection of His messianic claims by the populace in Galilee, including His final rejection in Nazareth spoken of as "His own country," caused Christ to withdraw from the unbelieving crowds and focus His attention on faithful followers to whom He would give further instruction concerning the kingdom of heaven.

1. *Death of the Baptist* (14:1-12)

In his palace at Perea, far to the south of Capernaum, Herod was too far removed from the Jewish population to have immediately appreciated the reputation of Jesus when it was first publicly proclaimed. But later his thoughts were captured and his imagination began to work. He concluded that Jesus was John the Baptist risen from the dead. The *Herod* mentioned here and everywhere in the gospels, except in Matthew 2:1-19 and Luke 1:5, was the ruler of Galilee and Perea from A.D. 4 to 39. His full name was Herod Antipas. He was the son of Herod the Great by Malthace, a Samaritan. Herodias, daughter of Aristobulus, another son of Herod the Great by Mariame I, had married Philip, a private Roman citizen[1] who was another half-brother of Herod Antipas. Herodias was both niece and sister-in-law to Herod. Marriage to a brother's wife, much less a niece, was forbidden by Leviticus 18:16 apart from levirate marriage (cf. Deut.

---

1. F. F. Bruce. *St. Matthew* (Grand Rapids: Eerdmans, 1970), 48.

25:5ff). Herod's divorce and incestuous marriage to Herodias
was repeatedly condemned by John in the typical fashion of
an Old Testament prophet. Many believed John was a prophet, and they strongly disliked Herod Antipas (cf. 14:5; 21:26).
For those reasons Herod had been reluctant to kill John
(v. 5). The martyrdom of John was much earlier than the account in verses 1-2. Verses 3-12 provide a historical parenthesis, interjected by Matthew to make the story of Messiah's
herald (John) complete and to prepare us for the final rejection of Messiah Himself.

The daughter of Herodias greatly pleased Antipas at his
party. Although women were not expected to participate in
such affairs, the lust of the men sometimes encouraged such
entertainment (cf. Esther 1:3, 9-10; Dan. 5:1, 4, 23). Herod
was probably drunk when he first made the initial promise to
relinquish up to one-half his kingdom, and even more in-
ebriated when he agreed to give the girl John's head on a
platter. Antipas paid a price for his calloused immorality.
Aretas, King of Nabatean Arabs (cf. 2 Cor. 11:32), and father
of the woman Antipas had divorced to marry Herodias,
waged war against Antipas and defeated him. Antipas was
then banished to Gaul by Caligula, emperor of Rome.

The disciples who were allowed to visit John in prison (cf.
9:14; 11:1-3) also were allowed later to claim his body for
burial. Their report to Jesus would lead us to conclude that
they believed in Him and that His answer sent back to John
(11:4-19) encouraged John's waning faith.

2. *Feeding the Five Thousand* (14:13-21)

Many consider this to be the greatest of Christ's miracles. It
is the only one of the thirty-five recorded miracles to be
reported in all four gospels. Jesus did not want the encum-
brance of Herod's interest, so the report that Herod now
thought Him to be John the Baptist resurrected was enough
to encourage Jesus to leave the territory. The desert place
(v. 13) is an uninhabited location on the northeast shore of
the Sea of Galilee, probably within a mile of Bethsaida-Julias,

which was out of Herod's jurisdiction. There Christ might be able to rest and instruct His disciples who had just returned from their mission. However, a crowd anxious for a liberator had observed Christ embarking by boat and walked around the northern tip of the sea to find Him. When Jesus came forth from a secluded place near the hill where He had been with His disciples, His heart was moved by the needs of the throng, and He healed the sick.

For Christ, every human need was an opportunity to help and instruct, and He met the physical needs of the throng for those two purposes. His disciples, called to be shepherds of Messiah's flock, were prone to neglect that responsibility (cf. Matt. 14:15; 15:23). They needed to be reminded of their responsibility (v. 16) and their inability to discharge it in their own strength (v. 17). Christ tested His disciples' understanding by asking them how the needs of the crowd could be met (cf. John 6:5-6). He then illuminated their understanding by showing them how all human needs are ultimately met: He takes natural human ability (v. 17) and expands it by His grace and through His power and for His purposes (vv. 18-21). Matthew displays Jesus as the second Moses, the prophet of the end time (cf. Deut. 18:15-19). "There is first century evidence for the Jewish expectation that the gift of manna would be renewed when Messiah was revealed,"[2] For the first time John unites with Matthew's account and develops the spiritual meaning of the miracle (cf. John 6:26-58). Christ, the fulfiller of Old Testament prophecy (cf. 1 Kings 17:16; 2 Kings 4:43-44) is, as the divine giver, more important than the gift (cf. John 6:32). Do we go to Him for the supernatural help necessary to minister to His sheep?

3. *Walking on Water* (14:22-33)

Having experienced one of Christ's greatest miracles, the crowd enthusiastically sought to take Him by force and make Him king (John 6:15). Possibly to keep His disciples from be-

---

2. Ibid., 49.

ing swept up into that wave of misapplied excitement, Christ
compelled them to embark on a journey to the other side of
the lake (v. 22). After dismissing the crowd that was doubtless
reluctant to leave, Christ retired to a secluded place for
private communion with His Father (v. 23). While He was
praying, His disciples were rowing against a storm that bat-
tered their boat (v. 24) and allowed them only three or four
miles progress after about six to ten hours (cf. John 6:19).
The disciples were still several miles from shore and probably
near the point of exhaustion when Christ appeared and
walked toward them on the water. He would have walked by
(Mark 6:48) but they were terrified, thinking that they were
seeing a ghost, so He spoke to them and identified Himself.

Peter's response, found only here in Matthew, is an
evidence of relief produced by faith in Christ's word, "Take
courage, it is I; do not be afraid" (v. 27). It was only when
Peter took his eyes and mind off the Lord and focused on the
raging sea that he began to sink. Imminent disaster ignited
new and desperate faith, and Peter's cry for help immediately
brought the needed salvation (v. 30). As Christ and Peter
entered the boat, the storm ceased and the boat was
simultaneously at shore (v. 32: John 6:21). The miracle ignited a worshipful response (v. 33) and the informal, spon-
taneous confession of the deity of Christ (v. 33; cf. Matt.
3:17; 8:29). The obvious purpose of the miracle was to increase the faith of the disciples. For centuries Christians have
acknowledged the practical lessons from this historical event:
first, the will of God sometimes leads disciples into difficulties; second, focusing on Christ releases supernatural
power enabling disciples to walk with Him amidst the storms
of life, whereas focusing primarily on the difficulties robs
disciples of the ability to be imitators of Christ (cf. 1 Cor.
11:1); third, when faith fails, a cry for help brings deliverance
(Heb. 4:16).

4. Healing in Gennesaret (14:34-36)

So widespread was the recognition of Christ's healing

power that shortly after disembarking from the boat at Gennesaret (a densely populated fertile plane south of Capernaum), word was sent throughout the towns and villages in the area that He was back. The sick came to be healed. It was not the superstitious touch of the tassel of His garment that healed, but rather the power and love of Christ responding in mercy to their needs that transformed them to health. For similar circumstances note Matthew 4:24, 8:16, and 9:20-21.

5. *Ceremonial Versus Moral Defilement* (15:1-20)

Sometime after Christ returned to Herod's territory, scribes and Pharisees from Jerusalem (Mark 7:1-2) joined forces with those of like mind in Galilee to discredit Him by asserting that His disciples did not keep the traditions of the elders relative to ceremonial handwashing (vv. 1-2). The "tradition of the elders" was their explanation of how the commands of God were to be lived out. Because such explanations were supposedly more understandable than the biblical text, breaking those explanations was deserving of greater punishment than disobeying the text. According to the Talmud, "to be against the words of the Scribes is more punishable than to be against the word of the Bible."[3] Ceremonial washing of hands, referred to in this passage, was commanded only for special situations (Lev. 15:11; cf. 16:26, 28). Nowhere in the Old Testament is it stated that such a ceremony must always precede each meal.

Christ responded to their barbed question with a devastating rhetorical reply, "Why do you yourselves transgress the commandment of God for the sake of your tradition?" (v. 3). Giving one example, Christ showed that their *corban* tradition voided the unqualified divine injunction that men should honor their parents under all circumstances (cf. Ex. 20:12; 21:17; Deut. 5:16). The heavy burden of having to bestow honor on parents by supporting them was being

---

3. William Hendriksen. *Exposition of the Gospel According to Matthew* (Grand Rapids: Baker, 1975), 614, as quoted from the *Talmud* edited by A. T. Robertson, 150.

CORBAN" - GIFT TO GOD.

neglected by the practice of promising one's property to God. Such property was "corban" (a gift). No matter how thoughtlessly uttered, the promise had to be kept. Although one's parents might starve, the vow was not to be broken. It is even suggested that what was *corban* could be used by the man for his own comfort and enjoyment, apparently under the guise that his work as a scribe or Pharisee was God's work.

Christ's crushing denunciation follows in verses 7-9. Such frustration of divine edict is seen to fulfill Isaiah's condemnation of his contemporaries who paid lip service to God but failed to render Him heart obedience (Isa. 29:13). The gospels do not suggest, however, that all Pharisees were such hypocrites (cf. Luke 23:50).

Turning from His critics, Jesus asked the crowd to come closer to "hear, and understand" (vv. 10-11). The Pharisees taught that the touch of a hand, which was ceremonially unclean, would defile the food, which in turn would make the eater unclean and open the door to demon possession.[4] Jesus asserted that defilement was conveyed not by ceremonial neglect (food entering a man), but by morally evil thought, what comes out of man's *mouth* (i.e., *heart,* cf. v. 18). The defilement that matters is ethical, not ritual.

That the Pharisees understood Christ's denunciation is related in verses 12-14. Jesus and His disciples were in the house (Mark 7:17). The disciples conveyed that the Pharisees were offended. They were literally shocked, for Christ's revolutionary statement cut the very ground of their teaching from under their feet. If the words of God ranked infinitely higher than the traditions of the elders (cf. vv. 3, 6, 9) and the people were to understand that, then the rule of elders would be ended (vv. 13-14). Christ did not soften His statements against the Pharisees; instead, He pronounced their ultimate judgment (v. 13; cf. Matt. 13:24-30) and asserted that they should be abandoned (v. 14).

---

4. Oswald J. Sanders. *Bible Studies in Matthew's Gospel* (Grand Rapids: Zondervan, 1975), 84-85.

Peter asked for a further explanation (vv. 15-20) of the parable (cf. v. 11). After rebuking him for lack of spiritual insight (v. 16), Christ went on to observe that what goes into the mouth passes into the stomach and is eliminated. In no way does it involve the heart and, therefore, cannot defile the heart. But what comes out of the mouth proceeds from the heart and gives rise to a variety of sinful words and deeds that break the sixth, seventh, eighth, and ninth commandments. *Wicked schemes* (v. 19) are literally *wicked deliberations.* Christ reiterated His cataclysmic statement in verse 20. The Messiah, who was Himself the Truth, was being progressively rejected. Perhaps we should ask in what ways we may excuse ourselves from God-given responsibilities under the self-deluded guise of piety while proudly upholding the traditions of the Christian community. Do we reject the Truth?

6. *Healing of the Canaanite Woman's Daughter* (15:21-28)

Christ's public Galilean campaign (4:12—15:20) had come to a close. Apart from a limited ministry in Perea (15:21—20:34) the Messiah retired from public ministry (v. 21). But even the seclusion of a house (Mark 7:24) was insufficient to keep Him from being discovered. Testimony of His Person and work had preceded Him to the area (cf. Mark 3:8). A Gentile woman, a descendent of Syrophonecians of Canaan, came to Him with a desperate need. Her daughter was demon-possessed! Her poignant plea (v. 22) and steadfastness amidst seeming refusal (vv. 23-26) reflected the kind of character that Messiah desired of kingdom participants and brought the reward of answered prayer and praise in verses 27-28.

The woman's agony for her daughter was constant. Love and empathy made the girl's illness as difficult as if the mother herself were ill. Knowledge of who Jesus was produced sincere reverence for Him, which enabled her to call Him "the Son of David," (i.e., the Messiah, v. 22) and to worship Him (v. 25). That the disciples attempted to hinder her prayer, and that the Lord at first remained silent (v. 23) and then seemingly rebuked her prayer as not "proper" (v. 24) did not contradict what the woman knew of Christ's character, nor could it deter her desperation. Nowhere in Scripture do we see Christ ultimately refusing an earnest, humble, and sincere appeal for help. Here, as elsewhere, the Lord may have delayed in answering her request to strengthen her faith (cf. John 11:13-15; Rom. 4:18-21).

The triumph of the woman's faith is seen in verses 27 and 28. Note how her humble spirit released a quick wit enabling her to seize on the positive side of the Lord's statement. To be compared to a pet dog (v. 26) is much better than being compared to a wild, vicious street dog (cf. 7:6; Phil. 3:2). A good master has affection for his household pets and will not allow them to starve. "Crumbs" from the Lord's table are all that she needs. This woman was an Israelite in the truest sense and a sincere believer. Twice Matthew records accounts of the exemplary character of specific Gentiles, in which faith turned the Lord from His preeminent work in Israel to heal Gentile loved ones from a great distance (cf. 8:5-13). But only after Christ's death and resurrection would the door be open wide to Gentiles (cf. Acts 10:34-48). Amazingly, Jesus bestowed the gift of faith and then extolled the recipient of such faith for exercising that which He alone had made possible.

7. *A Multitude Is Healed and Four Thousand Are Fed* (15:29-39)

Jesus continued to preview His ministry to the Gentile world by exercising authority over infirm bodies and great hunger. How long He stayed in the region of Tyre and Sidon is not known. In returning to the shores of the Sea of Galilee, He avoided the territory of Herod Antipas and chose instead Decapolis, the league of ten cities, a largely Gentile region under Herod Philip's jurisdiction (v. 29: Mark 7:31).

When the news spread that He was in the area, many afflicted with handicaps were brought and laid at His feet. Although the Messiah had sought seclusion and an opportunity to teach His disciples, His compassionate nature would not refuse meeting the needs of the crowd (vv. 29-31). This is probably a case of many miracles being performed simultaneously. Again the prophecy of Isaiah 35:5-10 is recalled. During the three days (v. 32) Christ must have instructed the people in the way of life. There is, however, no indication that any believed He was the Son of God after the miracles were performed. That the multitude praised and glorified "the God of Israel" may be further indication that they were not Israelites, but Gentiles (v. 31).

This entire passage represents a close parallel to Matthew 14:13-22. In both passages the sick were brought to Him, healed, and miraculously fed. Some scholars have suggested that Matthew and Mark mistook one account of a miraculous feeding for two accounts. However, the dissimilarities between the two events are numerous. The first feeding was near Bethsaida and ministered to five thousand Jewish men in the spring when they could sit on "grass." After one day of a healing ministry, five loaves and two fish were utilized. Twelve "baskets" of food were left over after everyone was fed. Christ then *sent* His disciples across the sea toward Capernaum. The second miracle was in the area of Decapolis, involving four thousand men, primarily Gentiles, who were seated on grassless ground in summer. It was after three days of a healing ministry that seven loaves and a few fish were multiplied so that all were fed and seven "hampers" of food were left over. (Such a hamper was large enough to conceal Paul in his escape from Damascus, Acts 9:25.) Christ then accompanied His disciples to Magdala or Dalmanutha (Mark 8:10), an unknown location on the western shore. The fact that these are two separate miraculous feedings is ultimately clarified by the distinction that Christ made between them in 16:9-10.

What are the spiritual lessons? First, to provide only for the family of Israel is insufficient; Christ is the "bread of life" for the whole world. Second, His disciples are to be His intermediaries; He takes all that man has to offer and miraculously multiplies it to meet the need, however great!

8. *A Second Request for a Sign Brings a Warning Against the Leaven of Unbelief* (16:1-12)

After returning to the more densely populated and mostly Jewish western shore, Jesus is again confronted by His bitter opponents (vv. 1-4). Matthew joins the Pharisees and the Sadducees together more frequently than the other New Testament writers. Those religious parties, usually at odds with each other, tempted Jesus to produce a "sign from heaven" (v. 1). The request was an attempt to invalidate all of Christ's miracles and to discredit Him publicly by revealing His failure to produce an absolutely compelling sign on demand. It was a hypocritical, impertinent, and insulting request that brought Christ's ministry in Galilee to a climax. He had already fulfilled prophecy attributed to Messiah, spoken the words of God, and proved His character. His emphasis on the grace and love of God rather than on man-made, culture-bound regulations, and His demonstration of authority over all of creation clarified the inadequacy of legalism and foretold its downfall.

Christ knew that the religious leaders saw Him as a theological and political threat. He denounced their hypocritical attitude and chastened them for being unable to interpret the spiritual signs of the times. Anyone who claimed to be a spiritual leader should have been able to read the significance of current events. The greatest sign of all stood right in their midst (cf. Matt. 24:30; John 1:14). Events that would have a dramatic effect on their lives were taking place. The word *times* (*kairon*) is used in the New Testament to speak of epoch-making periods in history and does not stress the idea of *change* so much as it stresses the idea of *contrast*. Those men did not recognize that their superficial quibblings robbed their attention of the critical issues of life. Their unbelief was not because of a lack of evidence, but because of an absence of spiritual perception, a deadness of heart. The sign of Jonah, which would be given them, is not explained here as previously done (12:38-40). Jonah's experience with the sea creature was a prefigurement of the death and resurrection of

Christ. The greatest sign was yet to come: Christ's atoning death and glorious resurrection would triumph completely over His enemies and prove Him to be Messiah (Rom. 1:4).

Having left His antagonists, Christ embarked with His disciples to the eastern or northeastern shore of the lake (v. 4). Upon arrival His disciples discovered they had forgotten to bring food (v. 5) except for one loaf of bread (Mark 8:14). As they were reflecting on their lack of food, Jesus warned them to beware of the pernicious evil (cf. v. 4) of the Sadducees and Pharisees, the unbelief that He described as leaven (v. 6). Christ was not referring to a set of doctrines but to an attitude of rejection toward the Spirit's ministry through Him. As *leaven* or *yeast,* those religionists would increasingly infect the lives of others. The disciples thought that Jesus was rebuking them for forgetting to bring food (v. 2). Upon perceiving their thoughts, Christ rebuked them on two points (vv. 8-11). First, they should not have been worrying about food; He had already shown His ability to provide for their needs in abundance. Their lack of trust seemed already to be reflecting the work of unbelieving leaven (v. 8). Second, they were rebuked for their lack of spiritual insight; they should have understood that the leaven referred to the doctrine of unbelief taught by Christ's enemies. Messiah ever sought to instruct His disciples in the spiritual significance of the events of His life, and the disciples seemed slow to learn the lessons. After His rebuke and explanation, they understood (v. 12).

8

THE KING'S TEACHINGS

G. THE PERSON AND WORK OF THE MESSIAH (16:13—17:27)

On the outskirts of Caesarea Philippi, in the secluded regions about twenty-five miles north of the Sea of Galilee, Jesus created an opportunity to be alone with His disciples. It was then that previously veiled concepts of His suffering and death for the sins of the world were made clear (cf. 10:38—12:40).

1. *Peter's Confession to the King* (16:13-20)

For nearly three years, by the example of His life, the display of miracles, and His teaching, Jesus revealed Himself to His disciples as the Messiah, the predicted King, and the Son of God. Now, through the use of two carefully chosen questions, the thinking of His disciples would be clarified and confirmed. First, He asked them who men said that He, the "Son of Man," was (v. 13). The messianic title "Son of Man" used in Daniel 7:13-14, stresses the humanity of Messiah. In response, the disciples suggested three thoughtful answers that some perceptive observers of Christ had shared (v. 14). Some identified Jesus with John the Baptist (cf. 14:2), others thought He was Elijah (11:14; 17:10), while some said that He was Jeremiah (cf. Jer. 7:4; 11; Matt. 21:12-13; 24:2). None of those answers, so typical of man's attempt to solve the riddle of the Person of Christ without divine illumination, satisfied the Lord. So, He asked them the second and crucial question: "Who do you say that I am?" In the original Greek a strong emphasis is placed on the personal pronoun *you*. The question was addressed to the disciples (vv. 13, 15), and

Peter, spokesman for the group, responded for them. "Thou art the Christ" is their confession that He is Messiah. Andrew, Philip, and Nathanael had made similar confessions nearly three years earlier (John 1:41, 45, 49), but Jesus was so unlike the expected Messiah that they may have changed their minds. Peter's deliberate confession as contrasted to the sudden emotional claims on the storm-calmed sea (Matt. 8:27; 14:33) showed that the disciples' thinking was maturing to conform with what Jesus actually was and taught. By calling Jesus "the Son of the living God," Peter may have made the connection with Psalm 2:7, where the Father says of the Messiah, "Thou art My Son." The fact that Messiah is *the* Son of God contrasts Him with mere mortal man. He is the eternal Son who is God Himself. The concept of Christ's deity must have been just dawning on the consciousness of the disciples.

In answering Peter (vv. 17-19) the Lord was also speaking to the other apostles. He called Peter *blessed* because Peter's understanding that Jesus was the promised Messiah, the unique Son of God, was a direct result of divine illumination. All who believe as Peter believed are "blessed" of the Father (cf. Rom. 8:29-30).

In the first of four assertions, Jesus addressed Simon Barjona as "Peter" (Greek word for *rock*). The insecure apostle would become stable in faith. Using a play on words in His second assertion, the Lord told Peter that He would build His church upon "this rock" (v. 18a). Historically, there have been four basic interpretations of that statement,[1] ranging from the contention that Peter is the *rock* and the church will be built uniquely upon him, to the conclusion that Peter's *confession* is the rock upon which the church will be built and that Peter himself is insignificant. As Howard Vos affirms, Peter (*petros* in Greek) is masculine for a piece of stone "which as the classics show a Greek warrior sometimes ob-

---

1. William Hendriksen. *Exposition of the Gospel According to Matthew* (Grand Rapids: Baker, 1975), 645-49.

tained by sticking the top of his sword into a ledge of rock, a *petra,* and twisting it. Thus the petros is part of the petra.''[2]

Peter was the first among equals, and the church would be built upon him only in the sense that as a recipient of God's grace He had received divine illumination, faith in Christ, which He would share. Although he was the most significant of men in the beginning of the church, Peter would not stand alone. The other apostles would also be used by Christ to lay the foundation of His church (cf. Eph. 2:20). The book of Acts records the history of that foundation. In the absolute sense, it was Christ Himself who was the foundation or rock (1 Cor. 10:4) upon which Peter and the other apostles stood (1 Cor. 3:11). The beginning of the unique New Testament church, the *Body of Christ,* has its historical genesis in Acts 2.

3　　Christ's third assertion (v. 18) is that ''the gates of Hades shall not overpower'' the church. As Vine affirms, the term ''Hades'' is probably derived from *hado,* signifying ''all receiving'' and speaks of the abode of all dead, equivalent to *Sheol* in the Old Testament.[3] It seems consistent with the text to interpret ''the gates of Hades'' as figurative language for death itself. Death, the greatest and final enemy, will not hinder the ultimate victory of the church (cf. 1 Cor. 15:3-4, 26, 54-57). The power of death, which seems to be the ultimate assault against the church, might appear to win some temporary victories, as martyrs' blood spilled for two thousand years attests, but the church marches on. With the provisional death and resurrection of Christ the greatest hindrance to God's plan for man has been overcome. All lesser forces of evil are also ineffectual (John 16:33; Eph. 6:10-13; Rev. 20:7-10), for all power in heaven and on earth belongs to the Head of the church—Jesus Christ, the Messiah! (Matt. 28:19; Phil. 1:6).

4　　Christ's fourth assertion to Peter is that He will give him

---

2. Howard F. Vos. *Matthew: A Study Guide Commentary* (Grand Rapids: Zondervan, 1979), 120.

3. W. E. Vine. *Expository Dictionary of New Testament Words* (London: Oliphants, 1958), 187.

the "keys of the kingdom of heaven" (v. 19*a*). Keys were a sign of authority, the ability to open to others the truths of God's kingdom (cf. Isa. 22:22: Rev. 1:8; 3:7). To insert the key and open the doors of the kingdom of heaven would be literally to preach the gospel. Peter was uniquely privileged to open the door of the kingdom of heaven to Jews (Acts 2) and to Gentiles (Acts 10:1—11:18; 14:27; 15:7, 14). Those "keys" were given to the other apostles (Matt. 28:18-20; 24:14; Mark 16:15; Acts 1:8; 10:42) and to all Christians (2 Tim. 2:2; 1 Pet. 3:15; 2 Cor. 5:20; Rom. 10:11-16; Eph. 6:15; Matt. 28:18-20).

Finally, in verse 19*b* Messiah related that whatever Peter "shall bind on earth shall have been bound in heaven, and whatever [he] shall loose on earth shall have been loosed in heaven." In rabbinical usage the power to bind was the authority to impose an obligation and the power to loose was to negate any such obligation. "Heaven, not the apostles, initiates all binding and loosing, while the apostles announce these things."[4] Here kingdom standards of conduct are in view. Peter, in reflecting God's mind, had derived authority. That authority also was given to the other apostles (Matt. 18:18) and to the church (28:18-20). The Jerusalem Council (Acts 15) seemed to reflect such authority. In John 20:22-23, that privilege is related to forgiveness of sins. On the basis of God's Word, those who preach the gospel have the authority to assert that those who receive Christ are forgiven.

Jesus' warning that they "should tell no one that He was the Christ" (v. 20) must have been given because the multitude was not yet ready for the truth. Note previous admonitions to secrecy (Matt. 8:4; 9:30; 22:16). Christ was not about to become their political "messiah."

2. *Messiah Prophesies His Death and Resurrection* (16:21-28)

Following the momentous confession of Peter, a turning

---

4. Charles C. Ryrie. *Ryrie Study Bible* (NASB) (Chicago: Moody, 1976), 1474.

point in the gospels, Christ began to predict clearly His
special ministry as Savior. Early hints of His commission to
die had been partially veiled (cf. Matt. 9:15; 12:40; John 2:19;
3:12-16; 6:45-51). Unclouded assertions would help the disciples to understand (v. 21; cf. Matt. 17:22-23; 20:18-19) if
not immediately, at least after His resurrection appearances.
Messiah *must* be involved in a series of four events to fulfill
His prophesied mission: (1) He must go to Jerusalem, the
Holy City (Matt. 4:5; 5:35), where His formal presentation
was to take place (Matt. 21:1-11; Luke 13:33); (2) He must
suffer many things from the elders, chief priests, and scribes,
the three groups that made up the Jewish "Supreme Court,"
the Sanhedrin. That formal judicial body had the responsibility of accepting or rejecting messianic claims on behalf of
the nation; (3) Christ must die, for only through His death
could the key to the kingdom be made; there could be no
good news of forgiveness without the judgment first being
borne (2 Cor. 5:21); and (4) He must be raised up on the third
day to verify His office as Savior, continue His work as Great
High Priest, be prepared to reign over all creation as King of
kings and Lord of lords and remain true to His Word (Rom.
3:4; 1 Cor. 15:3-4; Rev. 19:11-16).

Peter's reaction (v. 22) showed that he did not make a complete transition from what his nation commonly expected of
Messiah to what Christ taught about Himself. Very few Jews,
if any, expected a suffering Messiah. The general concept was
of a victorious conqueror who would break the shackles of
Rome from their backs. Peter's rebuke of Christ contained
the assumption that Christ was wrong, that the heavenly
Father would not allow that to happen to His Son. Peter
meant well; he wanted his Messiah to be enthroned and
honored, not humiliated.

Christ's rebuke of Peter (v. 23) is a stark contrast to His
early commendation (vv. 16-18). Peter the *rock* had become
Peter the *stumbling stone,* or *trap.* Jesus did not mean that
Peter was Satan, but that urging Christ to shrink from death
was siding with Satan's plan, not God's (cf. Matt. 4:8-9).

To be a good disciple of the King, one must *take up* ("pick up at once") his cross and bear it after Christ (v. 24). That crossbearing is symbolic language for voluntary submission to the discipline necessary for becoming more like the King. It includes denying fleshly ambitions or desires and seeking after those attitudes and actions that are more of a reflection of Him (cf. 1 Cor. 9:24-27; Gal. 2:20). Following the Messiah would be more than a minor inconvenience, for the *cross* is also representative of the suffering that accompanies following Christ: the servant is not greater than his master (Matt. 10:38-42; John 13:16).

Christ encourages men to make the right choice and follow Him, for He desires that they experience fuller, freer, and truer lives (v. 25). "Whoever wishes to save his life" [that is, keep it from the King's authority] "shall lose it; but whoever loses his life for My sake" [that is, subject one's life to the authority of the King] "shall find it" (cf. John 10:10). Ultimate personal integration is only possible when the Author of life is accepted, worshiped, and followed as the Ruler of life. Many decisions that would otherwise seem foolish are made desirable "for Christ's sake" (Matt. 22:37; John 14:21). Christ further encourages men to follow Him by asking a rhetorical question (v. 26). The word "forfeit" refers to the loss of true life through deception or fraud. Those who do not follow with the King have been defrauded of the opportunity to become what they were intended to be. The terms "life" and "soul," used interchangeably in verses 25-26, are actually the same word in the original Greek. What shall a man give in exchange for himself? Nothing, for no exchange is possible. His choice is to lose everything or surrender his life to God.

Every man will be "recompensed" according to his "deeds", or conduct (v. 27). There will be degrees of reward for believers (1 Cor. 3:12-14) and degrees of punishment for those who reject Christ (Rev. 10:11-15) at His return. The relative degree of rewards or punishment is based on the amount of knowledge (i.e., light) concerning Christ and His

kingdom that a person has received (Rom. 2:12) and how that
knowledge has been used (Matt. 23:14; Luke 12:47-48).
Christ was not talking about salvation from sin's penalty, for
that is totally dependent on acceptance of Him as Savior-
God.

Christ's coming to render each according to his deeds (v. 27)
and His coming in royal dignity (kingship, v. 28) are closely
related, but not identical. Jesus may have been using prophetic foreshortening to describe the final consummation of His
program in verse 27 and the beginning of the last phrase in
verse 28. Christ was certain of His final victory and symbolized it in various ways. "The apocalyptic eschatological sym-
bolism employed by Jesus here does not dominate His
teaching. He used it at times to picture the triumph of the
kingdom, not to set forth the full teaching about it. . . .
There would be climaxes and consummations."[5] The coming
described in verse 28 did not necessarily have to take place
during the lifetime of the disciples listening to Him, although
several of them would receive a sneak preview of the majesty
and power of Christ that would be manifested at Christ's second coming (Matt. 17:1-13; cf. 2 Pet. 1:16-21).

3. *Transfiguration of the King* (17:1-13)

The three disciples closest to the Messiah—Peter, James,
and John—ascended a spur of Mount Hermon with Christ
and there witnessed a conversation among Jesus, Moses, and
Elijah (vv. 1-3; Luke 9:32). What the disciples saw would
forever be imbedded in their memories (cf. 1 Pet. 1:16-17).
Jesus was transfigured before their eyes; they saw in advance
the Lord's "body of His glory" (Phil. 3:21), a body that He
did not permanently utilize until the resurrection (1 Cor.
15:40-44). As God, Messiah cannot change (Heb. 13:8), but
as man He did change. Here, as His body experienced
metamorphosis, His essence became more visible, irradiating

---

5. A. T. Robertson. *Word Pictures in the New Testament,* (Nashville:
Broadman, 1930), 1:138.

His entire being. "His face shone like the sun, and His garments became white as light" (v. 2). That was innate glory manifested in Jesus, in contrast to the residue of God's glory reflected from Moses (Ex. 34:33-35). Moses, here representing the Old Testament law, and Elijah, representing the prophets (Luke 24:44), were well-equipped to intelligently discuss their topic of conversation (v. 3), the death that Messiah would "accomplish" (Luke 9:31).

When Peter saw that Moses and Elijah were leaving (Luke 9:33), he attempted to prolong their visit by suggesting they make tabernacles (or booths) for their evening comfort. While Peter was still speaking, the *Shekinah* glory of God cast a shadow on them (cf. Ex. 16:10; 40:35), and the voice of the Father interrupted him. The same statement that encouraged Jesus at His baptismal (Matt. 3:17) scene also encouraged Him here prior to His passion. Although the disciples were terrified by the cloud and the voice and fell on their faces (v. 6; cf. Isa. 6:5), their faith in Christ's deity was confirmed (cf. Matt. 16:16). To comfort the men He loved, Jesus tenderly touched them and encouraged them to stop being afraid (cf. Matt. 9:2; 14:27; 18:10). When the disciples looked up, Jesus had resumed His normal appearance, and the cloud, Moses, and Elijah were gone. Christ's admonition to tell no one of the event until after His resurrection protected their privacy from the intrusion of excitable crowds until the proper time (28:19-20).

The appearance of Elijah was a reminder to the disciples of the scribal teaching that Messiah's coming would be preceded by Elijah (Mal. 4:5-6). That nonfulfillment of prophecy was puzzling. Jesus asserted that Elijah was to come before Messiah, but that he had already come in the sense that the same spirit that called for repentance and spiritual reform evidenced in Elijah was found in John the Baptist (Matt. 11:14; Luke 1:15, 17; 3:12-18). Spiritual blindness prevented the scribes from perceiving that figurative fulfillment and they killed John. Although the disciples understood that (v. 13), they seemed blind or unwilling to understand that their Messiah, too, must die (v. 9*b*, 12*b*, 16:22) before the glory, which they briefly observed, would be His forever.

All true followers of the King are in the process of being *transfigured,* being inwardly changed by the Spirit of God (cf. 2 Cor. 3:18), and are admonished to seek such a metamorphosis (Rom. 12:2).

4. *The King Heals a Demon-Possessed Boy* (17:14-21)

Reminiscent of when He left His home in glory to take the body of a man and suffer in a fallen world, Christ left the glory of the mountaintop to minister to a fallen, broken, and sin-sick world below. The day after His transfiguration, Jesus discovered the other nine disciples in debate with scribes (Luke 9:37). On approaching the group, the father of a sick boy came to Him, fell on his knees, and begged for mercy for his son. That the boy often fell into fire and water indicates epileptic fits or perhaps suicidal tendencies (cf. Mark 9:18, 20, 26; Luke 9:39), either or both of which had been caused by a demon.

Although Christ had given His disciples sufficient authority to perform miracles successfully in His name (Matt. 10:1, 8; Mark 6:13, 30; Luke 9:6), they were unable to perform this healing-exorcism (v. 16). Such circumstances demanded a rebuke from the King (v. 17). The "unbelieving and perverted generation" must have included more than the disciples, for all had demonstrated a lack of faith (cf. the father, Mark 9:24; the scribes, Mark 9:14; the multitude, 6:30; and the disciples, Mark 9:22-23). Their perverted perceptions of Christ kept them from complete trust in Him (cf. Deut. 32:5; Acts 12:45; 16:4). Sufficient evidence had been given to straighten out their thinking concerning the Person and power of Christ, but their neglect or rejection of that evidence now left their trust weak and caused Christ great anguish (v. 17).

Again the majesty of the King was demonstrated as He blamed and rebuked the demon for causing the illness of the child. The boy was instantly cured (v. 18; cf. Luke 9:43). A short while later (cf. Mark 9:28) the disciples asked why they were unable to heal the boy (v. 19). Christ's answer was that their faith was too small; even smaller than a mustard seed. Mustard-seed faith does not give up, but persists in prayer (Matt. 7:7-11), grows in the process (12:31-32), and ultimately sees the mountain removed. *Removing mountains* (v. 20) was an oriental idiom for removing difficulties (cf. Zech. 4:7). The promise that faith removes difficulties is not unequivocal, but rather is dependent on the believer's desiring to do God's will (cf. Phil. 4:13; James 4:3). Either the faith of the disciples had waned since their previous successes, or the demon was stronger than any they previously had faced. This was not the first time they were rebuked for lack of confidence in the King (cf. Matt. 8:26; 14:31; 16:8). Verse 21 is not found in some of the most authoritative manuscripts of Matthew, but is a true detail probably added from Mark 9:20 by a scribe.

5. *Second Prediction of the Death and Resurrection of the King* (17:22-23)

This second, clear-cut prediction of His death and resurrection emphasizes the certainty of the events (cf. Matt. 16:20). Private instruction for the disciples continued as "they were moving about together in Galilee."[6] The fact that He was about "to be delivered" stressed the nearness of His death and resurrection. Some ancient manuscripts suggest that the "gathering together" referred to small groups all over Galilee gathering for the purpose of preparing for the trip to Jerusalem and Passover. Although the disciples did not protest against the Lord's prediction (cf. Matt. 16:21), they did not fully understand it and were afraid to ask about it (cf. Mark 9:32; Luke 9:45). Their deep grief (v. 23) showed some understanding of His death without an equal understanding of His resurrection. That sorrow remained with them, and Jesus attempted to minister to their despondency on the last night of His earthly ministry (cf. John 16:6).

---

6. Hendriksen, 676.

6. *The King Pays the Temple Tax* (17:24-27)

Matthew is the only gospel that records this magnificent story of the King, which transpired on His return to Capernaum, a tax collection station. Peter was approached by a publican who was uncertain whether or not Jesus, who did not follow all Jewish customs, would pay the Temple tax (v. 24). The two-drachma tax, an average of two days' wages, was required by Mosaic law for the maintenance of the Temple (Ex. 30:11-16; 38:26; 2 Chron. 24:6, 9). Every Jewish male, twenty and over, paid the tax annually. Peter, possibly remembering the Lord's assertion that He came to fulfill the law (5:17-18), replied that His teacher would indeed pay. But Peter's answer may have been a little too flippant, for he apparently "intended to take up the matter with Jesus."[7] Jesus anticipated what Peter was going to say when they met, for He spoke first (literally, "went before Him"[8]) and asked Peter a thought-provoking question, which was also a rebuke. "Customs" were tariffs on goods, and *poll taxes* were taxes on persons.

Peter's acknowledgement that kings preferred to tax aliens rather than their own families led to Jesus' logical conclusion that "consequently the sons are exempt" (v. 26). So, a fortiori, the heavenly Father would not tax His own Son. The Temple belonged to Messiah's Father (John 2:16). Peter must also have known that the Son is greater than the Temple (12:6), the symbolic meeting place between God and man. The Temple tax was said to be a "ransom" for the soul to "make atonement" (Ex. 30:12, 15-16). Instead, He would give His life as an atonement, as a ransom for many.

Peter and the disciples were to understand that Christ was not contradicting His previous claims to be the Son of God by paying a Temple tax. Nor would He be the cause of encouraging others to disrespect the Temple and the law by misinterpreting why He did not pay a divinely instituted tax. With

7. Robertson, 1:143.
8. Ibid.

kingly condescension He waived His royal prerogative "lest [He] give them offense" (v. 27).

His command to Peter to "go to the sea" and catch a predesignated fish called attention to the King's omniscience and His sovereignty over creation. The fish presumably refers to a musht or combfish, which is prone to having "glittering objects in its gullet."[9] Because the *didrachma* was not in circulation at that time, there would be a *stater* (full sheckel) in the fish's mouth. It was worth twice the amount of the Temple tax for one man. Therefore, two men often paid the tax together with one coin.[10] This is the only miracle story in the gospels that leaves the reader to infer that the miracle occurred.[11]

9. F. F. Bruce. *St. Matthew* (Grand Rapids: Eerdmans, 1970), 59.

10. J. Oswald Sanders. *Bible Studies in Matthew's Gospel* (Grand Rapids: Zondervan, 1975), 97.

11. R. V. G. Tasker. *The Gospel According to St. Matthew* (Grand Rapids: Eerdmans, 1976), 171.

9

THE KING'S DISCOURSE ON HUMILITY AND FORGIVENESS

H. DISCOURSE ON HUMILITY AND FORGIVENESS BY THE KING (18:1-35)

This chapter presents another beautiful unit of Matthew's collection of Christ's teaching directly concerning the conduct of His disciples in the kingdom of heaven. Background for this discourse is found in Mark 9:33-34, where we read that the disciples argued over who would be the greatest in Christ's kingdom. Possibly the prominence of Peter (cf. chaps. 14—17) prompted the question. Greatness in the community will require humility (vv. 1-6), caring for the weak (vv. 7-14), correcting the wayward, (vv. 15-20), and continually forgiving one another (vv. 21-35). Fellowship with the King and His servants will be based on those qualities.

1. *Greatest in the Kingdom of Heaven* (18:1-6)

Apparently Jesus had been speaking privately with Peter, but "at that time" (v. 1) other disciples who had been arguing on their way to the house, joined them. Their heated discussion concerning who would be the greatest in His kingdom was known by the omniscient Christ, who prodded them to ask their question openly (Luke 9:46-47; Mark 9:33-34).

To answer their question, Christ called to Himself one of the many children who were frequently around Him (cf. 14:21; 15:38; 18:3; 19:13, 24). This little boy who first stood at His side (Luke 9:47) and was then picked up in His arms (Mark 9:36) provided an excellent object lesson.

Christ dealt with the more important matter of how to enter the kingdom (v. 3) before He answered their question about who would be the greatest in the kingdom (v. 4). The attitude necessary to open the gate into the kingdom is the same attitude that needs to be maintained in the kingdom. A conversion, or change of mind, by which the individual honestly recognizes his own moral limitations and God's absolute righteousness and all-sufficiency are prerequisite. That attitude reorients one's life toward God. The significance of the death and resurrection of Christ on behalf of the individual has become clear (1 Cor. 15:1-4). The Spirit of God gives faith, confidence in Christ (Eph. 2:8-9). The individual is born again at the point of conversion (John 3:3) and becomes a spiritual child of the heavenly Father (John 1:12). For all time and eternity the child of God is to maintain a childlike attitude—not *childishness,* but a truthful humility that often is associated with childhood. Trust, openness, an eagerness to learn, unpretentiousness, and frankness are characteristics that every healthy believer will manifest as a consequence of God's work in his heart. The individual cannot change himself, for only by the work of the Spirit of God is such humility possible (cf. John 3:3; Jer. 31:18; see also Matt. 5:3-6; 20:20-28; 23:11-12). Those who are humbled by an appreciation of the greatness of God are the greatest in the kingdom because they reflect how great He is.

To receive or positively encourage such a person for Christ's sake is akin to receiving God, because such God-humbled people are His children and representatives (v. 5). On the contrary, to "cause one of [those] little ones . . . to stumble" (v. 6) is to cause that believer to sin. To be guilty of that is to stand in the way of God's will and sovereign purpose in making His children into the image of His Son. You cannot separate the Lord from those that are His own. Blessings will come to those who encourage His children, but His curse will accrue to any who hinder their growth. The figure of speech for judgment is conclusive: there can be no escape for one around whose neck was tied a millstone weighing several hun-

dred pounds and then dropped into the "depth of the sea"
(v. 6). Such a fate would be easier and better than that which
faces the unscrupulous character who has led one of God's
"little ones" into sin.

2. *Woe to the Stumbling Block* (18:7-14)

Opportunities to hinder disciples in their spiritual growth
will always be a part of the world scene, for "it is inevitable
that stumbling blocks come" (v. 7). But woe to those who
cause the stumbling. Here Christ preserved the delicate
balance between the inevitability of hindrances and the moral
culpability of those guilty of them. Severe self-discipline is required if one is to avoid being a stumbling block to others.
Christ stressed that point through the use of exaggerated
language in verses 8 and 9. When Scripture uses such figurative speech, one must be careful to identify the central point
and not overemphasize details. In this instance the principle is
that disciples, when necessary, must ruthlessly narrow the use
of their faculties (hyperbolically, cut off the hand [v. 8] and
pluck out the eyes [v. 9]) when tempted to hinder the growth
of self and others (v. 10; Rom. 14:7). The "eternal fire" (v. 8)
and the "fiery hell" (v. 9) refer to Gehenna, the place of eternal separation from God. That is an expansion of Matthew
5:29-30 and is a judgment on the "world" (i.e., those who
have rejected Christ). Surely a believer, delivered from that
ultimate curse by accepting the substitutionary death of
Christ, should not want to be a part of such irresponsible, sinful action. Arduous self-discipline (vv. 8-9) greatly curtails
the likelihood that a more mature disciple would despise "the
little ones" and cause them to stumble (v. 10). That they are
looked after by His angelic host is evidence that special care
for the young in the faith is very important to God. Verse 11
is not found in most of the significant ancient manuscripts
and is probably a scribal addition to the text from Luke
19:10.

One who has stumbled has "gone astray" from developing
a Christlike character, and the Good Shepherd goes after Him

to restore him to the correct path. That is the teaching of the parable in verses 11-14. The same imagery of lost sheep is used in Luke 15:3-7 but is there applied to those who have never had a personal relationship with Christ. In the present text Christ spoke of the joy of restoring a wandering member to the right way of the flock. As the sheep strays, the reflection of the Shepherd's character in his life is drastically curtailed and he *perishes* (i.e., trifles away; cf. 1 Cor. 3:15). However, the wandering sheep has not lost an ultimate place in the fold (i.e., the kingdom; cf. John 6:39).

3. *Confronting a Disciple Who Has Caused One to Stumble* (18:15-20)

In the Kingdom, it is inevitable that some disciples will become stumbling blocks to others. Therefore, Jesus instructed His followers how they should respond when caused to stumble. First, the one sinned against is responsible for privately confronting the sinner to bring conviction of wrongdoing and win his brother (v. 15). An attitude of humility and a gracious desire to help the brother rather than get even is prerequisite to such a confrontation (cf. Gal. 6:1; Lev. 19:17-18).

Second, the matter should be kept as confidential as possible. Only when the impenitent person refuses to acknowledge his wrong should others be told. The offended brother is to take two or three witnesses with him in a second attempt to help his brother (v. 16). If the person still refuses to repent, the matter should be brought to the attention of the entire church (v. 17, i.e., the local fellowship of believers, not the universal church of Matt. 16:18). The church should further evaluate the matter to determine whether it can be established that the individual has grieviously sinned against his brother (Deut. 19:15). After careful, prayerful evaluation of the facts in light of Scripture, the church either binds the matter, disallows the deed, and declares the person guilty; or the matter is *loosed* (i.e., permitted) and the person is exonerated from wrongdoing. If the church's decision is based on what

God has already stated in His Word, God will have already ratified the decision of the church (v. 18; literally, "it shall have been bound . . . loosed in heaven"). If, when confronted by the local church, the offender still refuses to recognize his sin, the convicted person voluntarily excludes himself from the fellowship of his brethren. Consequently, he is to be considered an outsider (v. 17; cf. 1 Cor. 5:5). Note that the authority first given to Peter in Matthew 16:19 is here extended to the whole body of believers.

The necessity for prayer to precede such disciplinary action is emphasized in verses 19-20. The two or three witnesses of verse 16 should be united in prayer (vv. 19-20). The word "agree" carries the idea of making a symphony. When the Holy Spirit binds minds together on a specific issue, the answer is secure (cf. John 15:7). The promise of the Father to answer Spirit-directed prayer (v. 19) and the promise of the presence of Christ wherever the smallest group of believers gathers (v. 20), though here referring to disciplinary action, have a wider application and are a source of encouragement to believers.

4. *Always Forgive Your Brother* (18:21-35)

After Christ's teaching concerning winning a brother who has caused one to stumble (vv. 15-20), Peter had a question: How often should he forgive one who had sinned against him? To *forgive* means to cancel the right to demand a just penalty. Rabbinic teaching suggested three times (Amos 1:3; Job 33:28-30), but Peter had a clearer understanding of grace and thought that seven times would be adequate.

The Lord's reply stresses both the unfathomable depth of God's grace (cf. Eph. 2:1-10) and that forgiveness is to be a continuous state of mind (v. 22). "Seventy times seven" is not to be taken literally; that is, we are not to keep track of how often they forgive. Christ was figuratively stating that those who have been limitlessly forgiven should limitlessly forgive. The Christian community is based on forgiveness from God and must reflect His forgiveness, or its unique basis for fellowship with God and man evaporates.

In His hyperbolic parable (vv. 23-34), found only in Matthew, Messiah illustrated and logically confirmed His assertion. The story is of an ungrateful servant, probably a tax collector, who had been forgiven by his king for a huge debt that he could never have repaid. The servant refused even to be merciful to a fellow servant and defer payment on a trifling debt worth approximately one six hundred-thousandth of what he had owed the king. Such a hateful spirit was an insult to the example set by the merciful king and revealed a lack of understanding and appreciation for the king's gracious act. The dullard was disciplined until, it is implied, he realized the enormity of his stupidity and once more sought forgiveness. In learning gratitude he would learn to forgive (Eph. 5:18-20).

Christ emphatically concludes in verse 35 that so also will God deal with us if we do not limitlessly forgive each other. To forgive others is to honor what Christ has done for us. "Our sin debt to God was so horrendous and so totally beyond our ability to pay or to atone for that the sins which others commit against us pale by comparison."[1] What we really do know and appreciate of Christ's grace, we share (James 2:17-20). When children of the King do not forgive others, they must be chastened (Heb. 12:1-16; 1 Cor. 11:30-32) until the basic teachings of Christ are better understood and appreciated (Eph. 4:31-32). Learning is evident when disciples seek forgiveness for an unforgiving spirit. Christ concluded His retirement ministry with this series of lessons on conduct in what Bruce has called "one of the greatest chapters in the New Testament."[2] The King correctly anticipated the most difficult hindrance to fellowship among His disciples and attempted to prepare them for overcoming it.

---

1. Howard F. Vos. *A Study Guide Commentary* (Grand Rapids: Zondervan, 1979), 130-31.

2. F. F. Bruce. *St. Matthew* (Grand Rapids: Eerdmans, 1970), 61.

10

THE KING'S PEREAN JOURNEY

I. JOURNEY THROUGH PEREA (19:1—20:34)

Christ had completed His preresurrection ministry in Galilee. Multitudes, possibly on their way to celebrate Passover, were allowed to accompany the King and His disciples from Galilee, through Perea, and to Jerusalem. Matthew 19:1 refers to the area east of Judea across the Jordan River, which is Perea. Galileans often followed that route to avoid Samaria. During the journey, Christ continued to teach His disciples both by example and discourse. Matthew's coverage of this period omits a number of events (cf. John 7:8-10; 10:22, 39; 11:1-46, 54) to reemphasize previous teaching concerning life in the kingdom: marriage and divorce; the cost of discipleship; rewards in the kingdom; His death and resurrection; rank in the kingdom; and physical miracles. In many respects, the lessons taught and the miracles performed paralleled Christ's ministry in Galilee.

1. *Marriage and Divorce in the Kingdom* (19:3-12)

Once again the jealous Pharisees displayed their ever-increasing hostility. By confronting Christ with a barbed question about divorce, over which the people were divided, they had hoped to tempt Him and hinder His public testimony before the multitude. Some held that a man could divorce his wife for the most trivial of reasons, for "any cause at all" (v. 3). The less popular view held that divorce was only possible in cases of adultery. The test question for Jesus was, Did He agree with the liberal or the conservative school? In answering, Jesus referred to Genesis 1:27 (v. 4) and 2:24 (v. 5) and showed that God's purpose in creating a distinct male and a distinct female was to bring them together to make them one flesh; that is, a spiritual, emotional, and physical unity. Christ continued that marriage had been instituted by God and is "what God . . . has joined together" (v. 6). Therefore, a marriage annulment is in contradiction to the will of God, "let no man separate." The Pharisees countered with what they thought was a contradictory statement from the law of Moses (cf. Deut. 24:1-4): if God intended that there be no divorce, what then was the purpose of the "certificate of divorcement?" (v. 7). Their question, far from being perceptive, displayed a gross misunderstanding. The certificate of divorcement was not an escape clause from the marital contract, but a legal protection for women that formalized the act of divorce and obviated any capricious attempt to disannul a marriage. Christ, with characteristic understanding of the purpose of the law, replied (v. 8) that the allowance for divorce was a concession, not a commandment, made through Moses because of man's sinfulness; that is, a provision made after and as a result of the Fall of man. Divorce, He implicitly stated, goes against God's intent that marriage be both lifelong and monogamous and, at best, is the lesser of two evils when the ideal has been violated and irreparably damaged. Although it was not assumed or encouraged, divorce was allowed for "immorality" (v. 9). Here immorality means physical adultery. The Old Testament equivalent term had various interpretations from mere improper behavior or something offensive to physical adultery and even spiritual adultery (cf. Hos. 6:10; Rev. 19:2). Christ's point was that divorce is to be allowed for only the most severe abridgment of the marital bond, such as adultery. In New Testament times, a divorced woman may have been forced into a life of adultery.[1]

Having been defeated, the Pharisees apparently left and

1. R. V. G. Tasker. *The Gospel According to St. Matthew* (Grand Rapids: Eerdmans, 1976), 182.

Jesus and His disciples entered a house where the issue of marriage in the kingdom was to continue (cf. Mark 10:10). When the disciples, who were imbued with the lax attitude of their culture toward marriage, understood the very binding nature of the marriage bond, they questioned Christ as to whether it would be preferable to remain unmarried rather than to face a lifetime with an unpleasant partner (v. 10). Christ's response that "not all . . . can accept this statement, but only those to whom it has been given" (v. 11), although variously interpreted, seems to mean that only by God's grace are the eyes of fallen man opened to the perception of what marriage as a divine institution requires. First there is an obligation to God, and second, responsibility to the marital partner (cf. vv. 5-6). Christ concluded in verse 12 that it is better for some not to marry, for the ability to marry is a gift from God (cf. 1 Cor. 7:7). Some were not born with the ability to marry; others were inhumanely castrated; whereas still others chose to remain single for the sake of the ministry (cf. 1 Cor. 7:8, 24, 32-35). The latter were "eunuchs for the sake of the kingdom" (v. 12). Marriage would, however, be the normal expectation of every disciple. Not all would be able to comprehend what Christ said, but those who did needed to "accept it"; that is, personally practice what they had learned.

The Pharisees' barbed questions revealed a superficial understanding of scriptural morality based on the letter of the law. Their application of Mosaic law, although not always totally wrong, was inadequate. In answering them, Christ always pointed to the principles upon which the law was *based,* and thereby He transcended their wooden legalism to reveal the heart and mind of God (cf. Matt. 9:10-13; 22:15-22). The law stated that divorce was permissible. The first principle we find is that because marriage was ordained by God, it should not be annulled. Man should not sin, but because he does, God in His grace has made provision. Therefore divorce is permissible when, because of sin, the marriage bond is broken. The marriage bond is to present to the world and to believers a symbol of the beautiful love relationship between Christ, the Bridegroom, and the church, the bride (Eph. 5:32; Rev. 19:7).

2. *Blessing a Childlike Attitude in the Kingdom* (19:13-15)

It is fitting that Christ's statements regarding marriage and divorce should be followed by this incident concerning children who were brought to Christ for a blessing. Of the synoptics, only Luke does not follow this order (cf. Mark 10:13-16; Luke 18:15-17). The sanctity of marriage secures a blessing for children. Why the disciples attempted to hinder Christ's attention toward these children is unclear, but Christ's rebuke of the disciples for their action and His love for the children is abundantly clear. The children illustrate the simple, trusting attitude that is a prerequisite for entering Christ's kingdom (cf. Matt. 18:1-4). "Eternal life is practically synonymous with 'The Kingdom of Heaven,' to enter one is to enter the other (cf. Mark 9:43, 45 with 47)."[2] Compare also Matthew 19:16, 23-26.

3. *The Cost of Entering the Kingdom* (19:16-26)

Through a series of questions and answers Matthew relates the story of a wealthy young inquirer who was brought from a point of ignorance to a fuller understanding of the cost of entering the kingdom. Many Jews believed that a single heroic act, some kind of *work,* would open the door to salvation. That is apparently the thought behind the question of verse 16: "What good thing shall I do that I may obtain eternal life?" Christ chided the wealthy young man, seemingly unconvinced of his absolute sincerity (v. 17), before telling him that to "enter into life" he must "keep the commandments" (cf. Lev. 18:5; Deut. 30:15-20). Because the rabbis taught so many commandments, some said to be more important than others, the young man was not sure which commandments He meant (v. 18).

---

2. F. F. Bruce. *St. Matthew* (Grand Rapids: Eerdmans, 1970), 62.

Christ responded by mentioning five of the ten moral commandments from the Mosaic law—ones that dealt specifically with a person's relationship with his fellow man, summed up in Leviticus 19:18 (cf. Matt. 22:39). Revealing his immature self-knowledge, the young man claimed to have kept all those commandments and then asked what he still needed to do. He knew that even with wealth, youth, and position (cf. Luke 18:18) he did not have the satisfying life that was available (v. 20). Like Paul, he claimed to be blameless in observing legal righteousness (cf. Phil. 3:6). Christ loved this man who had so many admirable qualities (Mark 10:21) and felt compelled to show him that earning salvation was beyond his ability. He needed to be convinced of his moral need. That could only be possible as he learned the difference between the letter and the spirit of the law. So Jesus responded by saying that he could have eternal life by selling all he had, giving the money to the poor, and then following Him. "This is an ad hoc commandment addressed to a particular person at a particular time guilty of covetousness, not a special way to elite holiness."[3] In place of temporal, material wealth he would then have treasure in heaven.

Christ was not teaching that salvation could be earned that way, because selling all and giving to the poor does not exhaust the meaning of the law of love (cf. 1 Cor. 13:3), but it would show that he had trusted in Christ and believed in His word. When the rich man understood the cost, he missed the principle and proved that he was not ready for salvation. Obviously, he had not kept all the commandments, for if he truly loved his neighbor as he claimed, he would have gladly sold what he had and given it to the poor (cf. vv. 19-20). "The one who does not love his brother whom he has seen, cannot love God who he has not seen" (1 John 4:20). Instead of finding salvation, the young slave to his possessions dejectedly went away, unwilling to release control of his wealth to the King. Christ had spoken to the heart of the young man's problem;

---

3. Tasker, 187.

he was an idolator who loved money more than God (Ex.
20:3). "None can claim to be righteous when judged by the
commandments as interpreted by Christ."[4] Our only hope is
to come to Him for grace. We must pay the cost of discipleship now and reap the rewards later. But the world tells us
to reap now and pay the cost later.

That incident became an object lesson for the disciples. The
climax to the lesson is that it is impossible for man, rich or
poor, favored or unfavored with this world's goods, to save
himself. Until the young man realized that he was a law-
breaker and could not meet the demands of God—he could
not be saved. But with God anything not contrary to His
character is possible (v. 26). The plan of salvation is a blessed
accomplishment of God that transcends human reasoning (cf.
Isa. 55:1-3, 8-11). All who would have life with God must
first recognize the impossibility of such a relationship based
on human effort alone. Only by the grace of God can anyone
be saved. Temporal success, instead of being a blessing is
often a blindfold preventing men from seeing both the value
and the means of salvation.

4. *Rewards in the Kingdom* (19:27-30)

Peter's response contrasted his action with the rich young
ruler and seemed to imply the question, "What are we going
to get for being so much better than him?" (v. 27). Yet, the
gracious reply from Christ made it clear that it was a good
question. In the "regeneration" (i.e., the Millennium), when
Christ will establish His visible kingdom, (cf. Acts 3:21; Rom.
8:22-23) the disciples will have positions of authority (v. 28).
All other followers will receive from God many times over
what they gave up in relationships and possessions in addition
to eternal life (v. 29). Relationships based on a common appreciation of Jesus Christ go deeper and grow stronger than
even natural family relationships without Him, and the blessings begin now (cf. Mark 10:30). In eternity unsatisfied yearn-

---

4. Charles R. Eerdman. *Matthew* (Philadelphia: Westminster, 1966), 178.

ings will find optimum compensation. The warning (v. 30) is
that those in positions of preeminence now may not have such
positions in the kingdom, and those who seem unimportant
today may have positions of prominence then. An outward
appearance of importance does not impress God (cf. 1 Sam.
16:7). The disciples needed to judge their motives for leadership (Matt. 18:1-4; 20:25-28); as there are degrees of punishment in hell (Luke 12:47), so also there will be degrees of
glory in heaven (1 Cor. 15:41).

5. *Parable of the Kingdom Workers* (20:1-16)

Peter's question in Matthew 19:27 generated this light but
definite rebuke against his eagerness for reward. Reward was
promised (vv. 27-28), but a spirit that prompted service for
the sake of such recompense rather than love needed check-
ing. In this parable, found only in Matthew, Christ amplified
the thought that God's way of determining rewards in the
kingdom is different from man's. Man bases a person's worth
on achievement and power, which is in radical opposition to
God's perspective. Peter was prone to use man's inappropriate criteria of evaluation. That kingdom rewards are
first based on God's grace, not man's merit (v. 14; cf. John
15:5), is the key thought of this parable. A willingness to

serve, given the opportunity, is of greater significance than
duration of service (vv. 6-7). Some have called this parable
the gospel of the penitent thief (Luke 23:38-43), for the
"eleventh-hour" laborers also entered late into the Master's
service, but enjoyed some of the same blessings that the early
workers enjoyed. They were even paid first (v. 9), possibly so
that the early morning laborers could observe the landlord's
grace. Thus, many who would be considered first on man's
scale of values will be at the bottom on the King's list, and
many who would be at the bottom of man's pay list will be at
the top of the King's list (v. 16; Matt. 19:30). The grumbling
of verse 11 echoes the voice of the older brother in the parable
of the prodigal son, in which jealousy rather than justice was
the key motive for complaint. Disciples are to beware of an
envious spirit.

6. *Positions of Honor in the Kingdom of God* (20:17-28)

Positions of special honor in the kingdom of God are being prepared for those who have followed the King's example of humble service. This principle of kingdom living is framed by the final prophecies of Christ's passion (vv. 17-19, 28). These prophecies give a more detailed account than the two previous ones (cf. Matt. 16:21; 17:22-23) and highlight Messiah's matchless heroism as He refused to flinch from His redemptive work in spite of all the agonies that awaited Him. Jesus is the ultimate example of service and consequent greatness. His resurrection enables the fruit of His service to live forever (v. 19).

The request of James and John for preeminent positions in the kingdom (vv. 20-21), made immediately after Christ's prophecy, underscored the insensitivity, lack of understanding, and self-seeking of His followers, which was in contrast to the King's self-sacrifice. Their mother, probably Salome, Mary's sister (Matt. 27:56; Mark 15:40), is said to raise the question (v. 20), but Mark 10:35-45 makes it clear that the disciples themselves were behind the question. That fact was certified by Christ's response that they, (plural *you,* v. 22) not just the mother, did not know what they (again a plural *you*) were asking for. Messiah's kingdom would be governed by a level of character above their immediate ability to perceive (Luke 18:34). Consequently, they did not understand the degree of spiritual maturity prerequisite to the highest positions of authority in the kingdom. The cup that Christ must drink (v. 22) refers to His passion experience (Matt. 26:39). "In the Old Testament idiom, 'drinking a cup' (i.e., its contents) means fully undergoing this or that experience, whether favorable (Ps. 16:5; 23:5) or unfavorable (Ps. 11:6; Isa. 51:17, 22)."[5] Therefore, when the brothers replied that they were indeed able to drink His cup (v. 22), their boast was hollow, for their ignorance precluded an intelligent answer. Jesus foretold that they would suffer (v. 23; cf. Acts 12:2;

5. William Hendriksen. *Exposition of the Gospel of Matthew* (Grand Rapids: Baker, 1975), 746.

Rev. 1:9), but He graciously left out any prophecy of their denial of Him on the night of His betrayal (Matt. 26:31, 56).

The anger of the other disciples toward the two brothers (v. 24) was apparently a result of their jealousy for those same special positions, for the explanation of kingdom greatness was now directed to all the disciples (v. 25), not just to James and John. Instead of castigating His followers, Jesus used their interest to reiterate gently (cf. Matt. 18:1-4; 19:14-21, 30; 20:16) a principle He had constantly lived before them. They still accepted the Gentile standard and equated greatness with the "exercise of authority" (v. 25). The terms "lord it over" and "exercise authority" can be paraphrased "threw their weight around." The disciples' wish for authority was based on those pagan concepts. But leaders in the kingdom would emulate the King, and His leadership was in exemplifying how to serve others. "Servant" (v. 26) means "*willing* servant" (i.e., deacon), and "slave" (v. 27) means "*willing* slave." Consequently, the only wish for rank that would give authority in the kingdom would be a wish for a place of humble service. "And the place of honor is not a reward or compensation for the service; the service is the honor."[6] As the ultimate example, Messiah would become a "ransom for many" (v. 28); that is, a payment in the place of or on behalf of many. That substitutionary nature of Christ's death is here described in phraseology similar to that found in Isaiah 53:4-6, 8, 11-12 (cf. 1 Pet. 1:18). "So the Son of Man rendered the lowliest and simultaneously the noblest service of all by becoming a 'ransom for many.' It is as His people's Savior that He receives highest honor, and the shameful cross to which He was fastened has become the object of His people's chief glorying (Gal. 6:14)."[7] Those who would have special honor with Him would follow His example. This great lesson would need repeating (cf. Luke 22:24-30).

---

6. Bruce, 65.
7. Ibid., 66.

7. *Healing of the Blind Man* (20:29-34)

Just days before His agonizing death and with an indescribably heavy burden on His heart (cf. Matt. 20:17-19; Luke 12:5), Messiah graciously concerned Himself with the infinitely lesser burden of two blind beggars, whom He miraculously healed. Christ and His disciples left Perea, crossed the Jordan, and journeyed through old Jericho, approximately fifteen miles northeast of Jerusalem. A band of Passover pilgrims was accompanying them as they passed two blind beggars who made a plea for help. That the blind men called Jesus the Son of David placed a timely emphasis on His messianic calling and probably helped to prepare the crowds for His triumphal entry into Jerusalem (Matt. 21:1-11).

In spite of a stern rebuke from the multitude, the beggars continued to plead for mercy (v. 31). Mark and Luke stress that Christ responded to their faith (Mark 10:52; Luke 18:42); Matthew stresses that Jesus was "moved with compassion" for the plight of the blind beggars. Grace, love, and power are all seen in the King's response to the persevering and humble petition (v. 34).

Differences in the records of Matthew, Mark, and Luke show that there was no collusion among them to produce an artificial harmony in their stories. Each record is equally authentic and presents its own perspective under the inspiration of the Spirit of God. The gospel accounts of Mark and Luke include only one of the blind men, "Bartimaeus"; apparently because he was the vocal leader of the two. Most likely the healing took place as Jesus and the disciples were leaving old Jericho and about to enter new Jericho. (For other views, see William Hendriksen, *Exposition of the Gospel According to Matthew*, pp. 752-53.)

That beautiful example of humble, glorious service by the King ends the Perean ministry and the second main division of the gospel.

11

THE KING'S REJECTION

J. REJECTION OF THE KING (21:1—23:39)

Messiah's public ministry sufficiently validated His claim to be the king of the Jews and proved Him to be the Son of God. Yet, the reader anticipates the rejection by those to whom most of Messiah's ministry had been addressed. This section begins with triumph as the crowd proclaimed Jesus as Messiah, but soon records the rejection of the King and ends with Christ severely castigating the religious leaders for misleading the people.

1. *The King's Presentation at the Triumphal Entry* (21:1-11)

On Sunday of the passion week, Jesus went to the place where the Messiah was expected to appear (cf. Zech. 14:9), most likely the Mount of Olives near Jerusalem, although the exact location is not known (v. 1). There He would formally present Himself to Israel as the prophesied Messiah of Isaiah 62:11 and Zechariah 9:9. The Messiah was to enter Jerusalem, riding on the colt of a donkey (v. 5). In referring to those Old Testament passages, Matthew shows familiarity with the Septuagint, but he favors the Hebrew text. His explicit reference to both animals and his specific designation of the colt as a donkey makes his description of the event more comprehensive than the other New Testament accounts (Mark 11:1-10; Luke 19:29-40; John 12:12-19). That is in keeping with Matthew's more frequent and definitive use of Old Testament passages. Christ's first coming to Israel was in meekness and peace, on a lowly beast of burden, and resulted in national rejection, suffering, death, and resurrection. His second coming will be in power, to judge, physically conquer (Rev. 19:11-16), and will result in acceptance by the reborn nation and Messiah's eternal reign.

When the disciples returned from their errand (vv. 1-2, 6) they laid their garments on both animals, unsure of which one Christ would mount. An alternate reading of verse 7 denotes that they laid their garments on *it* (the colt) instead of on *them* (both animals).[1] By spreading their garments on the road (v. 8), special reverence was shown to Messiah (cf. 2 Kings 9:13). The tree branches and clothing kept the dust down as the unusual processional made its way toward Jerusalem. Cries of jubilation reflected the appreciation of Christ's miracles and the pregnant hope of a military-political deliverance from Roman oppressors. "Hosanna" is an anglicized form of the Hebrew word that means "save now," or "save, we pray." In calling Jesus the Son of David the people were publicly proclaiming Him the messianic king, an extolling of the Person of Christ that He refused to silence (Luke 19:39-40). "Blessed is the one who comes in the name of the Lord" is from Psalm 118-26, one of the six most quoted psalms in the New Testament. Psalm 118 is a messianic passage that was sung as an expression of high spiritual expectation, a "processional according to the Targum and Talmud, connected with the feast of Tabernacles and the close of Passover."[2] Israel looked forward to singing it at the "postulated autumn festival of enthronement in which the Davidic King, symbolically put in jeopardy by his foes, is delivered by the Lord and restored to Kingship."[3] How fittingly it was applied to Jesus!

But praise from the crowd was short-lived; even the disciples did not understand the event as it transpired (John

---

1. R. V. G. Tasker. *The Gospel According to St. Matthew* (Grand Rapids: Eerdmans, 1976), 198.

2. R. E. Nixon. "Matthew," *The New Bible Commentary,* rev. ed. Edited by D. Guthrie, J. A. Moyer, A. M. Stibbs, and D. J. Wiseman (Grand Rapids: Eerdmans, 1970), 525.

3. Ibid.

12:16). Although the city was in a stir over His unusual arrival
and many questioned who He was, word was circulated that
He was the prophet from Nazareth of Galilee (v. 11), hardly a
strong assertion that He was Messiah. Christ recognized their
misconception of His Person and kingdom and was brought
to tears when He saw Jerusalem (Luke 19:41-44).

2. *Cleansing of the Temple* (21:12-17)

Jesus exercised His messianic prerogative and cast out
fraudulent money changers and thieving sacrifice vendors
from the Temple court of the Gentiles. Operating under the
authority of Annas, the robber and ex-high priest whose son-
in-law Caiaphas ruled as the high priest, the "bazaar,"
charged exhorbitant prices for sacrifices—as much as four
dollars for the purchase of a pair of doves worth about five
cents outside the Temple. A change of coin to pay the Temple
tax cost a twenty-five percent commission.[4] The noisy, sor-
did, legalized stealing from sincere worshipers at the center of
Judaism symbolized the hypocrisy of the priests and the kind
of religious fraud that would come under the ultimate judgment of Christ. This was the second time Christ freed the
Temple of the parasitic perversion (cf. John 2:13-17).

The purpose of the Temple, as Jesus made clear by quoting
from Isaiah 56:7, was to provide a place for interaction between Jehovah and His people, a place of worship and
fellowship in connection with sacrifice. What Jehovah intended to be a "house of prayer" had been changed by the
religious leaders into a "den of robbers." What was true of
Judah in Jeremiah's day, just before the fall of Jerusalem (cf.
Jer. 7:11), had repeated itself in Christ's day.

Apparently the Temple police were unable or unwilling to
stop Christ's bold work; He was popular with the multitude
and the bazaar was very unpopular. The people themselves
would cleanse the Temple of that abuse in A.D. 67.[5]

---

4. William Hendriksen. *Exposition of the Gospel of Matthew* (Grand
   Rapids: Baker, 1975), 762.
5. Ibid., 770.

Only Matthew records that Messiah again proved His authority to judge and show mercy amidst righteous indignation by healing the infirmities of people who had been previously banned from the Temple (v. 14). Excited children repeated the refrain heard at the triumphal entry, "Hosanna to the Son of David" (v. 15), and as a result faced the indignation of the chief priests and scribes. With a reference to Psalm 8:2, a messianic passage He applied to Himself, Christ defended the children's worship. If adults would not praise Messiah, God would bring forth praise for Him from the mouths of babes. The entire psalm depicts the unlimited rule that Messiah would ultimately exercise as King. Jesus then returned to Bethany (v. 17), apparently His home base during the Passover week.

Since our bodies are the temple of the Holy Spirit (1 Cor. 6:19), we are given the choice to cleanse ourselves or be cleansed by the Lord (1 Cor. 11:30-31).

3. *Israel's Judgment Prophesied* (21:18-22)

On Christ's walk from Bethany to Jerusalem His anger appeared to be kindled when He came to an apparently healthy, fertile fig tree that gave the pretense of bearing fruit. Upon inspection the tree was found to lack the buds that develop into figs. The tree would not produce. Christ's physical hunger directed His attention to the tree, but His anger was against Israel, which gave promise of spiritual fruit by its religious foliage, but was barren of real fruit production. The tree provided a convenient and dynamic object lesson. In prophesying that the fig tree would wither, Jesus prophesied the ensuing judgment on Israel.[6] The Holy City literally would fall in A.D. 70. Soon after He spoke of the fig tree, Christ cleansed the Temple. Was the bazaar of Annas on His mind when He examined the fig tree?

Judaism viewed the fig tree as a symbol of prosperity

---

6. A. T. Robertson. *Word Pictures in the New Testament,* vol. 1, *Matthew* (Nashville: Broadman, 1930), 1:169.

(Deut. 8:8) and its destruction as a symbol of judgment (Hos. 2:12). Israel was supposed to receive her Messiah joyously; instead she was rejecting Him. Thus, the kingdom of God would be taken away from Israel and given to a nation that would produce fruit (Matt. 21:43). Without repentence, Israel would perish like a "fruitless fig tree" (Luke 13:1-9) condemned to be cut down and thrown away. (See also Judg. 9:8-12; Isa. 5; Jer. 24; Hos. 9:10, 16.)

Mark gives the chronology of the event, showing that Christ condemned the tree Monday morning and that it was Tuesday morning on their way back to Jerusalem that the disciples noticed the tree had already withered (Mark 11:11-12, 19-20). The words "at once" in Matthew 21:19, 20, referring to the duration of time between Christ's prophecy and the fulfillment, are better translated "soon," or "presently" in this context. Between the prophecy and the fulfillment, Christ cleansed the Temple. It is clear that the story could be handled topically, (as in Matthew), or chronologically (as in Mark).[7]

The disciples focused on the rapidity with which Christ's prediction came true rather than on the lesson that *privilege scorned* will be *privilege lost*. Seizing their interest, so as to teach another lesson, Christ instructed them that faith is the key to accomplishing miraculous things. The promise that "in all things you ask in prayer, believing, you shall receive" (v. 22) is unmodified when understood to mean that the petitioner is asking in the will of God. Christ was not here giving a discourse on prayer, but rather magnifying the power of God. All sincere petition begins with an appreciation of God's ability to act. "Removing mountains" (v. 21) was a common Jewish saying (cf. 1 Cor. 13:2) and often applied to the solving of difficult moral problems.[8] Jesus proved His power in both the physical and moral worlds. Prayer is an avenue through which God loans His power to the believer so

---

7. Hendriksen, 773.
8. Oswald J. Sanders. *Bible Studies in Matthew's Gospel* (Grand Rapids: Zondervan, 1975), 114.

that he or she has the ability to accomplish what ought to be done. And prayer enables God to do for us what we cannot do for ourselves.

The Mount of Olives, which will be split apart at the second coming of the Messiah (Zech. 14:4), was in view when Christ spoke of a mountain being removed (v. 21). Before Messiah could return to earth, disciples would have to exercise faith in Him and become fishers of men. The last man caught will be the final "catch" before His second coming. "Even" (v. 21) the establishment of Messiah's kingdom will be enhanced by faith.

4. *Religious Hierarchy Questions Messiah's Authority* (21:23-27)

As Jesus taught in the Temple He was interrupted by representatives of the Sanhedrin. Authorization for teaching and other religious activities came from that prestigious body. The representatives asked Christ where He got His authority to do "these things" (v. 23); that is, teach, cleanse the Temple (12-17), and so on. Once again their intent was to deny His authority and publicly humiliate Him. Even a sign from heaven (Matt. 12:38; 16:1) would not have convinced them that Jesus was the Messiah.

Aware of that malicious design, Jesus posed a question of His own (vv. 24-25): Was the baptism (i.e., the ministry) of John the Baptist from God or man? Jesus' question was actually an answer that forced the Sanhedrin to focus its attention on the evidence for His divine authority. John had been the prophesied way-preparer for the Messiah. To accept divine authorization of John's ministry would necessitate accepting Christ's divine authority, for John pointed to Jesus as to a superior (Matt. 3:11-12; John 1:26-34). If, on the other hand, Christ's antagonists had admitted that they did not believe John's ministry was of God, they would have lost the support of some people who revered John as a prophet of God (v. 26). Either alternative would have been costly for the religious hypocrites.

It was public knowledge that John's authority had been denied by most religious leaders, so when those representatives said they had no opinion or "did not know," they lied openly and publicly discredited their right to judge religious matters. Jesus had beat them at their foolish game: "Neither will I tell you by what authority I do these things" (v. 27). If they were incapable of judging John the Baptist, certainly they were not qualified to judge the Messiah.

5. *The Parable of Two Sons Condemns the Sanhedrin* (21:28-32)

Messiah did not allow His antagonists to get away. In the first of three parables Jesus confronted the religious leaders with the fact that their prideful claim of doing the will of God was mere pretense and that they would be excluded from the kingdom of God. Only by genuinely doing the will of God (Matt. 7:21-27), as did the converted tax collectors and prostitutes, would they be allowed to enter the kingdom.

In this parable, found only in Matthew, two sons were asked by their father to go to work in the vineyard. One son, apparently in a cordial way, said that he would do so, but did not. The second son was hostile and said no, but regretted not going and went anyway (vv. 28-30).

Jesus asked the religious leaders which of the sons did the will of the father, and their response set them up for the application (v. 31*a*).

Tax collectors in their greed and prostitutes in their sexual immorality had openly rebelled against the will of God but later repented under the preaching of John (v. 32; Luke 3:12). Their lives displayed faith that worked, John's "way of righteousness," and they would enter the kingdom of God *before* those religious leaders who yet needed to repent. Some had responded to John the Baptist (John 5:35), but had later rejected his message. Such dramatic change in the lives of the tax collectors and harlots (v. 21; cf. Luke 3:10-14) did not convince even those religionists of the veracity of John's message concerning Christ (v. 32).

Doing the will of God means to trust and follow the Lord Jesus Christ and encourage others to do the same (Matt. 3:2; 4:17; 28:19-20; John 6:29).

6. *Parable of the Wicked Vine-Growers* (21:33-46)

Successive details of this parable correspond so accurately with the successive points of reality that Christ made after the parable that it is almost like an allegory. Messiah continued His verbal attack by telling His enemies they would lose the privilege of representing God's kingdom and be crushed for their rejection of Him. Jesus' claim to deity and predictions of His crucifixion, resurrection, and coming judgment of those rulers became increasingly open and emphatic.

The story (vv. 33-39) is about a property owner (Jehovah), who leased a specially prepared vineyard (Israel, Isa. 5:7) to vine-growers (rulers of Israel). When the time came for the owner to collect rent, he sent his servants (Old Testament prophets, cf. Matt. 23:35, 37) to pick up his percentage of the fruits (or righteousness, v. 19). However, his servants were beaten, stoned, and killed. In an amazing display of patience and grace beyond measure, the Lord sent His son (Jesus Christ) to make the final attempt to collect the amount due. But the vine-growers took the son outside of the vineyard and killed him (the crucifixion of Jesus outside the city gates, Heb. 13:11-13).

Christ asked His enemies what should be done to such tenants. Reminiscent of King David's self-condemnation (2 Sam. 12:1-12) those men pronounced their own judgment (v. 41).

Jesus made His application crystal-clear (v. 42) by quoting Psalm 118:22-23, in which builders (probably leaders of the nations surrounding ancient Israel) had rejected a stone (symbol of the Davidic monarchy, Israel, and a messianic term, Isa. 28:16). But God took the scoffed nation and set her above the others (Ps. 147:20). That came about not by Israel's might, but by the power of the Lord (v. 42). Jesus then showed that He was the ultimate embodiment of true Israel.

Like the stone that was cast aside by heathen powers, He was to be cast aside by the chief priests, scribes, and their followers. But something marvelous would happen: the crucified Jesus would be resurrected and become the chief cornerstone of a new universal, invisible temple, the church (Eph. 2:19-22), made up of Jews and Gentiles who would worship God in spirit and truth.

As judgment had come upon the ancient Gentile powers, so also would God judge those religious rulers. Their privileged place with Him would be taken away (John 4:21-24) and given to a nation (the church, 1 Pet. 2:9) that would produce fruit (v. 43). All who come under the judgment of the Cornerstone (Christ, Acts 4:11-12) will be crushed (v. 44; Isa. 8:13-15). To emphasize judgment, Jesus left out any promise of a restored Israel.

Christ's antagonists clearly understood their public condemnation (v. 45). They would have seized Him, but His popularity with the pilgrims prevented them from doing that (v. 46). They heard His claim to be deity (the Son of God) and were aware that He knew of their plans to slay Him (John 11:47-53).

7. *Parable of the Marriage Feast* (22:1-14)

This is the third parable and is found only in Matthew. It reiterates the impending judgment of Israel for rejecting God's gracious invitation of salvation through Christ. Whereas others will enter the kingdom, Israel will be lost. To emphasize that rejection and judgment Messiah omitted any word of the repentance and faith that will bring on the future regathering of Israel. Since Christ does not interpret this parable for us, scholars have come up with various interpretations.[9]

The kingdom of heaven is pictured here as a festival and a wedding feast, a familiar image to the Jewish mind (cf. Isa. 25:6; 55:13; 61:10; 62:5). A king (God the Father) sent

---

9. Tasker, 206-8.

messengers (John the Baptist and the apostles before Christ's passion) to those ''who had been invited'' (Israel, through the Old Testament prophets, v. 3). But the Jews rejected that invitation. The king, according to oriental custom, sent another invitation. At this point, the meal ''had been prepared.'' That apparently is a prophecy of the gospel being preached to the Jews first, after Christ, our Passover (1 Cor. 5:7), was crucified, resurrected, and ascended. But the ingrates, previously indifferent to the king's invitation, became hostile. The persecution and murder of the messengers may refer to the suffering of the apostles and early Christians (Acts 7:59; 12:2). In response to such heinous treatment of the gracious bearers of his invitation, the king sent his armies. That may be a prophecy concerning the destruction of Jerusalem in A.D. 70 under Titus, when over a million Jews were killed and Jerusalem and her Temple were destroyed. Israel was to lose her identity as a political state for about 2,000 years. (For God's use of even heathen powers to further His purposes, cf. Prov. 21:1; Isa. 45:1; Jer. 25:9; Dan. 4:17.)

In verses 8-10 messengers went to the crossroads or ''main highways'' and gave an open invitation to all who would come. Although a number of Jews would enter the kingdom as a result, most of those entering would be Gentiles (Acts 22:21-22; Rom. 9; Matt. 8:11-12; 21:41). Both ''evil and good'' were invited and brought into the visible church of Jesus Christ (cf. 13:47-50) and ''the wedding hall was filled.'' Apparently, that is referring to the gospel going out into the whole world (Matt. 28:19-20; Acts 1:8).

But everyone who publicly professes faith in Christ does not necessarily accept His provision of forgiveness. The evil ones are probably those who attempt to enter God's kingdom on their own merit. Their best works are as ''filthy garments'' in the Lord's eyes (Isa. 64:6). The good apparently are those who have been clothed in the righteousness of Christ (Gal. 3:27, 11). Having been declared righteous (justified), their lives then produce righteousness (sanctification; Col. 3:8-14; Rev. 19:7-8). Eternal separation from God, the second death

(Rev. 20:6, 14) awaits those who claim to be Christians but have not accepted the gracious forgiveness of God (vv. 11-14). Thus, the man "not dressed in wedding clothes," not clothed in Christ's righteousness that comes by faith, is cast out. "Outer darkness" is in contrast to the light at the wedding feast (cf. John 8:12). That those who are refused a place in the kingdom will experience "weeping and gnashing of teeth" is evidence of their agony. They will have missed the purpose of their existence (cf. Matt. 8:12; 13:42, 50; 24:51; 25:30). Many are called to fellowship with God (v. 14), but few are "chosen" (Rom. 8:28-30).

8. *Messiah's Opponents Ask Him Three Barbed Questions* (22:15-40)

With anger and murder in their hearts, the religious leaders retreated from the sting of Christ's parables and planned another attack. If they could get Him to discredit Himself publicly, His popular support would be lost.

In verses 15-22, Matthew records the first of three questions addressed to Christ. Students of the Pharisees, the orthodox ecclesiastical group, joined forces with the Herodians, supporters of the Herods, a family granted political power in Palestine by Rome. Their question (v. 17) was shrewdly designed to force Christ either (1) to lose support of the orthodox community, whose members reasoned that because God had given them the land of Israel their allegiance should be to Him alone, without paying the tax collectors; or (2) to be accused by the Herodians of being a traitor and rebel to Rome and subject to crucifixion by standing against the tax (Luke 20:20; 23:2). Payment of the "poll-tax" (v. 7) required of every male adult who lived in Judea, was the "hottest political question of the day in Judea."[10] In answering their question, Christ cut throught their hypocrisy and malice (vv. 16-18) and showed the distinction yet interrelationship between what is called secular and sacred. "Render to Caesar

---

10. F. F. Bruce. *St. Matthew* (Grand Rapids: Eerdmans, 1970), 71.

the things that are Caesar's'' (v. 21*b*) means to repay a debt, not to give Caesar tribute as God. They accepted the coin with his image (v. 19) and thereby symbolically accepted the benefits of living under his government. They used and enjoyed both the technology and peace supplied by Rome. Therefore, they had to be willing to *render* (i.e., give back to Caesar what belonged to him for those services). It was God's will that the emperor be obeyed (Rom. 13:1-7) unless his laws were to clash with God's edicts (Acts 5:29). Christ added that they should also give back to God His due (21*b*). He was sovereign over *all,* which included the Roman government (see Dan. 4:34-35). The image of Caesar was on the coin; the image of God is on man. The coin belonged to Caesar; man belongs to God. Those thoughts were a revelation that so startled and confounded the antagonists that they left in amazement (v. 22). Not only had Messiah answered sincerely, but He had beaten them at their game, solved a riddle of practical living, and emphasized the central theme of His own teaching: give to man what is his due, but a higher allegiance belongs to God.

On that same day, the Sadducees had their only recorded direct confrontation with Christ (vv. 23-33). Their barbed question about life in the resurrection was founded on a rationalistic view of life and the rejection of any belief in angels, bodily resurrection, or an afterlife (Acts 23:8). They elevated the Pentateuch above the rest of the Old Testament and interpreted it literally. In quoting Deuteronomy 25:5 on what is called the *law of the levirate marriage* (marriage to a husband's brother, v. 24), they set the stage for a logical argument designed to discredit Jesus as a teacher by either showing the absurdity of the doctine of the resurrection or by causing Him to contradict the Mosaic law and prove Himself a heretic. Their illustration of the woman who was married successively to seven brothers as each preceding one died (vv. 25-28) was an accentuation of a true story. The clincher (v. 28) must have brought smirks to their faces: ''In the resurrection therefore whose wife of the seven shall she be?

For they all had her." The Sadducees were implying that because Moses established the levirate law, he could not have believed in a future life, much less a resurrected body, for the results would be ludicrous. The fallacy of their argument was in thinking that the future life will be like this life to the extent that conditions that prevail now will prevail then (e.g., marriage with copulation and procreation). According to Christ, their false presupposition was caused by two areas of ignorance: they did not understand the Scriptures; nor did they understand the power of God. First, as to their ignorance of Scripture, rather than relying on some proof-text for the resurrection (cf. Ps. 16:9-11; Isa. 26:19; Dan. 12:2; Hos. 6:2; 13:14), Messiah spoke of the essence of God and quoted from the Pentateuch to which the Sadducees referred. In Exodus 3:6 God speaks of Himself as presently being (i.e., "I Am"), the God of the patriarchs of Israel, who all had long since died. Because God is only the God of the living and is the God of the patriarchs, the patriarchs are alive. Jesus took it for granted that immortality assumed a bodily resurrection. Second, their whole question becomes irrelevant when one understands the implications of God's power and that the Scriptures teach that resurrected life is different from what we know in this life (1 Cor. 15:35-49). A levirate marriage was designed to provide the deceased with progeny to carry on his name and inherit his property (Deut. 25:5-10). But God's power has made possible a resurrection in which there is no death, and therefore, marriage as a procreative function will be unnecessary. A quality of relationships that surpasses any known on earth will prevail.

Jesus defeated their appeal to logic with His logic, which was based on fuller knowledge. Understandably, the multitude was astonished at His teaching (v. 33).

Having heard that the Sadducees were thwarted in their attempt to discredit Christ, the Pharisees, represented by one of their lawyers, presented what was to be their final public question to Him (vv. 34-40). Students and teachers debated on which of the 613 commands was the most important. No matter what answer Christ would give, some would disagree.

Messiah's answer was in two parts and based on Deuteronomy 6:5 (v. 37) and Leviticus 19:18 (v. 39). "You shall love the Lord your God with all your heart and . . . soul" was a verse quoted by all Jews in their daily prayers, and it required doing *all* His commandments (1 John 5:3*a*). By adding that one should also love his neighbor as himself and that all the law and prophets rested on those two commandments, Christ was saying that if you love God to the fullest extent of all your faculties, you will love your neighbor as yourself (v. 40; cf. Matt. 5:43-48; 6:1—7:12; Rom. 13:9-10; 1 Cor. 13). Apparently, Jesus was the first to combine those two texts to summarize the law as love. Dissimilarities found in the parallel passages in Mark 12:28-34 and Luke 10:25-37 have not been explained by literary source criticism and, rather than discrediting any account, seem to accentuate the authenticity of each writer's perception.

9. *Messiah Asks the Most Important Question* (22:41-46)

In this last public conversation with the Pharisees Jesus asked them a question that rendered their three questions insignificant. Christ raised the most important question that every human being must answer: "What do you think about the Christ, whose son is He?" (v. 42). An individual's answer to that question will determine his eternal destiny. Jesus designed the question to encourage recognition of Himself. The Pharisees' answer that Messiah was to be David's "son" (i.e., his descendent) was correct as far as it went (v. 42; 2 Sam. 7:12-13; Amos 9:13).

Next Christ raised a more difficult question: If the Christ is David's physical descendent, why does David call Him his superior, his Lord? To prove that David did call his descendent his Lord, Jesus quoted Psalm 110:1, a passage recognized by the Pharisees as composed by David under the influence of the Holy Spirit and referring to Messiah: "The Lord [Jehovah] says to my Lord [Messiah]: 'Sit at My right hand [position of special honor and authority], until I make Thine enemies a footstool for Thy feet.' " Throughout the New Testament, Psalm 110:1 is the principal passage quoted to show that Jesus is Lord and seated at the right hand of God (Acts 2:34; Rom. 8:34; 1 Cor. 15:25; Eph. 1:20; Col. 3:1; Heb. 1:13; 1 Pet. 3:22; Rev. 3:21).

The more complete answer to the question, Whose son is Messiah? is twofold: (1) He is the descendent of David, a human being, and (2) He is the Son of God: that is, God Himself. In this passage Jesus revealed the mystery of the hypostatic union, that He is one Person with both a divine and a human nature. He is undiminished deity and perfect humanity united in one Person forever. Scientists call two "proven" concepts that are unreconcilable an *antinomy* and work with the assumption that both are true. We cannot and should not expect to understand fully the two natures of Christ. His essence, although revealed, is incomprehensible to our human intelligence. Yet, we are to live in the light of the truth that He is God and man.

The Pharisees thought of Messiah as a human warrior rather than a divine Savior; they looked for a son of David who would display military might. It was time for their concept of Messiah to be expanded. Jesus showed that David's Son was also David's God, and thereby explained a difficult text.

Such a logical exposition of one of the key psalms silenced them. "No one was able to answer Him a word" (v. 46). Jesus won all of His public debates with the Pharisees and Sadducees, forcing them to operate underground.

10. *Messiah Condemns Religious Leaders* (23:1-39)

When one who is characterized by meekness becomes angry, we should take note. Matthew records the most scathing denunciation of the Pharisees found in the gospels, and here in Christ's fifth discourse, his commentary reaches a climax. Rabbinical writing enumerates seven kinds of Pharisees; six are negative and one positive: "he who is a Pharisee for love of God."[11] Nicodemus, Gamaliel, and Saul of Tarsus fit the

---

11. William Barclay, *The Gospel of Matthew* (Philadelphia: Westminster, 1958), 2:284.

latter category. Messiah satirized hypocrisy (pretending a relationship with God) and then pronounced seven woes as the religious hypocrite's fortune. But Christ's anger is not without compassion; only after their repeated refusal to respond did He predict their judgment.

The multitude and Christ's disciples are warned about the scribes and Pharisees in verses 1-12.

These Jewish leaders followed thousands of traditional, legalistic, man-made requirements that they elevated to the same place as Mosaic law. Although they themselves did not keep such demands because they found loopholes or escape clauses, they hypocritically demanded that the people keep them (vv. 1-4).

Christ called them "showmen" because they liked to be the center of attraction, to "do all their deeds to be noticed by men" instead of sharing love and mercy for the glory of God and the good of men. The phylacteries, little leather boxes containing parchment with four prayers from Exodus 13:1-10, 11:16, Deuteronomy 6:4-9, and 11:13-21, were intended by God to encourage sincere believers to remember His grace (Ex. 13:9). Devout Jews wore them on the left wrist and forehead while they prayed. But these ostentatious religious leaders wore oversized phylacteries to demonstrate their exemplary piety and contrast themselves with the people.

The long tassel or fringe on the four corners of the outer robe (cf. Num. 15:37-41; Deut. 22:12), intended to serve as a reminder of God and His commandments, were made obnoxiously large to call attention to the petitioner instead of to the God of the commandment. The idea of the fringe is perpetuated today in the Jewish prayer shawl.

The Pharisees' love for the seats of honor at banquets and in the synagogue (v. 6) also tipped their hand. To be recognized in the marketplace and to be called "Rabbi" (i.e., teacher or doctor of the law) was a special delight (v. 7). Jesus argued for a balanced use of titles of honor for both human fathers and human teachers, for all human authority is ultimately derived from God, the absolute Authority (see Eph. 4:11 and 2 Cor. 12:29).

In contrast to the ostentatious "superiority" of the scribes and Pharisees, the greatest servant of God is also the servant of his fellow man (vv. 11-12).

Seven woes follow in verses 13-36. Messiah predicted the end of those religious leaders. "Woe" means "alas for you" and is not a curse, but a statement of fact. Their end would be judgment. The first three woes stress wrong *teaching* and the last three stress wrong *action*. Wrong actions flow from perverted teaching.

FIRST WOE (vv. 13-14)

The Pharisees would not enter the kingdom of heaven. Although they *claimed* to be doing the will of God while publicly involved in ritual prayer, they invalidated their piety by unjustly and selfishly evicting helpless widows from their homes. Their condemnation would be greater (v. 14) than the condemnation of the unjust, who had a lesser understanding.

SECOND WOE (v. 15)

"Proselytes" were full converts to Judaism. Those proselytes converted to legalistic, hypocritical religious practice were twice as zealous for the perversions of God's grace and, therefore, more thoroughly depicted the attributes of hell's inhabitants than even the Pharisees and scribes. The converted may become the perverted.

"During his early days in Pretoria, Gandhi investigated Christianity, visiting a church on several Sundays. His conclusion: 'The congregation did not strike me as being . . . an assembly of devout souls; but rather to be worldly minded people going to church for recreation and *in conformity to custom*' "[12] (italics added). Too often the sins of the Pharisees are the sins of Christ's church.

---

12. Ibid., 2:254-55.

THIRD WOE (vv. 16-22)

Apparently Christ used satire here to depict the certainty of judgment. An unwarranted distinction was made between oaths that were binding and those that did not need to be regarded as binding because they were slightly different in form (cf. Matt. 5:33-37). Promises were broken on the pretense of a pseudo-legal point.

FOURTH WOE (vv. 23-24)

Judgment is assured. Although the Pharisees legalistically tithed even the tiny bits of cooking and medicinal herbs (cf. Lev. 27:30), they ignored activities at the top of God's hierarchy of responsibilities: doing justice, being merciful, and living by faith (cf. Mic. 6:8). Messiah's satire depicted the Pharisees as straining their wine through muslin gauze so as not to contaminate their beverage ceremonially by contact with a gnat and then joyfully swallowing a ceremonially unclean camel (Lev. 11:4). This is the "picture of a man who has lost all sense of moral proportion"[13] (cf. Matt. 7:3-5).

FIFTH WOE (vv. 25-26)

Because only the outside of their lives (cups) were clean while their hearts were filthy, judgment was sure. In practice, food or drink inside a cup may have been obtained unjustly, but that did not matter if the outside of the cup was ceremonially clean: the Pharisee would not contaminate himself. Christ's point is that if they lived justly, the ceremony would by comparison be superfluous, for the greater is subsumed by the lesser and the ceremony was to serve righteous living.

SIXTH WOE (vv. 27-28)

Judgment was coming because their lives were "like whitewashed tombs." Jewish tombs were clearly identified by

13. Ibid., 2:294.

whitewash so the pilgrims who came to the holy feasts would not defile themselves by accidentally touching them. They were beautiful on the outside, but contained corruption on the inside. In the same way, those leaders were beautifully pious on the outside, but inside they were full of sin.

SEVENTH WOE (vv. 29-36)

This last statement of judgment was made because of the scribes' and Pharisees' rejection of God's prophet. They claimed reverence for God's prophets who had been killed by their ancestors, and yet, would similarly kill the prophets God had sent and would send to them (cf. Acts 7:51-60; Matt. 3:7). Even Messiah would be slain. Their accumulation of guilt would be greater than that of their ancestors because of their greater enlightenment. Upon the religious leaders would "fall the guilt of all the righteous blood shed on earth, from the blood of righteous Abel to the blood of Zechariah, the son of Berechiah" (v. 36). The first book in the Hebrew Bible is Genesis, in which the death of Abel is recorded (Gen. 4:8), and the last book is Chronicles (divided into First and Second Chronicles in our English Bibles), where the death of Zechariah is recorded (cf. 2 Chron. 24:20-22). They would be charged guilty of performing murder, from the first to the last one in their Bible.

Christ's compassionate longsuffering is recorded in His "Lament over Jerusalem" (vv. 37-39). Although he recognized recalcitrance in Israel, He related His desire to protect and care for her as a hen cares for her chicks. But Jerusalem would not allow Him! Verse 39 seems to indicate that Christ will cease all public teaching until His second coming, when He will be recognized as Messiah (Zech. 12:10). Note the gradual departure of God's glory from the earlier Temple before its destruction by the Babylonians (Ezek 8:4; 9:3; 10:4, 18-22; 11:23).

12

THE KING'S PREDICTIONS

K. MESSIAH PREDICTS DESTRUCTION AND GLORY (24:1—25:46)

It was probably a Tuesday, late afternoon before Passover. The controversy with the Sadducees and Pharisees had already taken place. His public ministry ended, Christ left the Temple, an act symbolic of walking away from the Israel that had rejected Him. As He and His disciples passed through the Temple area, the disciples called His attention to the magnificence of the Temple structure (vv. 1-2). Jesus did not contradict their appreciation of its beauty, but astounded them with the prediction that it would be destroyed.

The destruction of the Temple and Jerusalem in A.D. 70 by the Romans would prefigure the judgment of the world by Messiah at His second coming at the end of the age.

A central thought in this passage is that believers are to be ready for His return. Because we do not know exactly when the Son of Man will return, we must continually be alert for Him (Matt. 24:4, 23, 25, 42, 44-51; 25:1-46).

Chapters 24 and 25 constitute Christ's great eschatological discourse called the Olivet Discourse, so named because it was delivered on the slope of the Mount of Olives. By the time Christ and the disciples had walked to the Mount of Olives, the disciples were ready to ask two questions: "When will these things" (i.e., the destruction of the Temple and accompanying events) be?" and "What will be the sign (i.e., the symbol) of Your coming at the end of the age?" (v. 3).

1. *Destruction After the Gospel Is Preached to All Nations* (24:3-14)

Jesus answered the first part of the second question first:

"What will be the sign of Your coming at the end of the age?" His answer was general enough to keep His followers walking in faith and specific enough to keep us alert. The "end shall come" after the gospel has been preached to all nations (v. 14). But with such an answer there is the danger of misunderstanding and the consequence of being led astray (vv. 4-5, 10-12). Many will claim to be the Christ (v. 5), and their credence will be enhanced by the many wars that will transpire between nations, which hints that the end is near (vv. 6-7). Earthquakes and famines in various and unlikely places will also hint of the coming judgment ("increased intensity portends increased imminency," (v. 7).[1] Believers will be hated and killed, the pressure becoming so great that some will deny the Lord, hate each other, and aid the persecution of Christians (vv. 9-10, 12). Along with the false Christs will appear false prophets encouraging many to turn away from the Lord (v. 12).

Apparently the "sin unto death" (1 John 5:14-21), not the "unpardonable sin," will be the fate of those believers who turn from Christ. But the one who "endures to the end" (i.e., through the persecution) "shall be saved" (v. 13), that is, experience the joy of joining with Christ in His victory. He "who endures" through those earthly persecutions will have been saved (i.e., physically delivered into His kingdom). Some believe that verse 13 teaches that Christians may lose their salvation by turning their back on the Lord. Although that is a possible interpretation, it seems more consistent with other Scriptures to deduce that all who are saved from sin's penalty (Eph. 1:7; 2:8-10) will be kept through sin's temptations. Though they fall and even may be taken home to heaven, they will not be utterly cast out from God's grace. "The reference is not to the salvation of the soul of the believer who endures persecution, but to his deliverance by the Lord's return."[2]

---

1. Howard F. Vos. *A Study Guide Commentary* (Grand Rapids: Zondervan, 1979), 161.
2. C. I. Scofield. *New Scofield Reference Bible* (Oxford U.: New York, 1967), 1034.

2. *Messiah Will Come Like a Flash of Lightning* (24:15-28)

Jesus became more specific as to what will precede the sign of the end of the age and what that sign of His second coming will be. The appearance of the "abomination of desolation," spoken of by Daniel (Dan. 9:27; 11:31; 12:11), is a specific, identifiable precursor to the end (see also Mark 13:14; 2 Thess. 2:4). Old Testament Scripture speaks of the abomination as that which defames the character of God (Deut. 29:16-17; 1 Kings 11:6-7). "Desolation" indicates the effect produced by the abomination.

Josephus, the Jewish historian, records that about 170 B.C. Antiochus Epiphanes broke a contract he had entered into with Judah and forbade the offering of the daily sacrifice. He entered the Holy of Holies and offered swine's flesh on the idol altar he had erected to the Olympian god Zeus—*a double abomination.*

Here Jesus prophesied a second application of Daniel's prophecy. Luke 21:20 tells us that the desolation in Jesus' mind was the presence of the Roman army in the Temple.

When the armies of the Roman general Titus reached Jerusalem, many Christians remembered Jesus' warning (vv. 17-20) and fled to Pella in the mountains of Perea for refuge and were delivered. Although many escaped, Josephus records that 1,100,000 were massacred. If God had not cut those days short, none would have survived. Thus, the mere shadow of the future judgment was expressed.

A third and ultimate desolation is yet to come, when the anti-Christ will set up His false worship in the Temple in Jerusalem (cf. Mark 13:14; 2 Thess. 2:4). He will demand that the whole world worship him. Resisters will be persecuted and martyred; thus their instructions to flee to safety and the prayer that their flight be not in the winter or on a Sabbath when they would be less prepared to flee. This period called the *Great Tribulation* will be the worst period of trial that the world will ever know (vv. 21-22). Until that time the world's problems will continue.

Prior to the ultimate Tribulation, many false messiahs will appear and perform miracles, possibly fooling even believers.

History has recorded thousands of such false prophets over the last 2,000 years, and deceivers will continue to appear until Messiah comes. Hence the warning not to be deceived (v. 26).

Christ's coming will be a surprise (vv. 27-28). We are not to know the day or the hour, but are to be ready moment by moment (v. 27). The depravity of man may be in view, as the carcass of man will be devoured by vultures (v. 28). That may be a reference to the carnage of the great battle of Armageddon (Rev. 19:17-19).

3. *Messiah's Coming Disclosed by a Blaze of Glory* (24:29-31)

Soon after the ultimate Tribulation there will come cataclysmic changes in the heavens: the sun will not give light and the moon will not reflect light. Heavenly bodies will "fall" and "the sign of the Son of Man" will appear. The sign is probably the Shekinah glory, a manifestation of Christ's magnificent character announcing His visible, bodily return. The tribes who rejected Him will mourn their error, while those who trusted in Him, "the elect," will be gathered to Him.

4. *Parables Illustrating Messiah's Second Coming* (24:32—25:30)

Each of these parables stresses the need to be prepared for Messiah's return. Because these are parables and not allegories, this single main point concerning preparedness is what is to be learned.

a. Parable of the Fig Tree (24:32-35)

Observance of the fig tree's pre-summer changes anticipates the approach of summer, and observance of the signs prior to Christ's coming anticipates His return. "This generation" (v. 34) can refer to a race or family. In this context, the terms refer to the Jewish race. Thus, the Jewish race would be preserved until Messiah returns, in spite of many persecutions. The pronouncements of Christ are absolutely certain to come to pass (v. 35). The wise will learn from nature and be prepared for His return.

b. Parable from the Days of Noah (24:36-42).

The Jewish people were familiar with how unexpectedly the heathen had been overtaken by the Flood in Noah's day. Noah's preaching of God's Word had been rejected. Unprepared, the people were consumed in judgment. So also, those who ignore the Word of God and do not prepare themselves for Messiah's return will meet swift, even unexpected judgment.

The unexpected timing and nature of Christ's return and judgment will separate those who even work closely together (vv. 40-41). The "one taken" is apparently delivered from judgment, as was Noah. The "one left," like the heathen, is lost in the destruction. The wise person will learn from history and be prepared.

c. Parable of the Unprepared Homeowner (24:43-44).

Just as a homeowner would prepare himself against thieves, so Messiah asserts, "you are to be ready too." Even though we do not know the hour of His expected return, we are to be prepared, for He *is* coming.

d. Parable of the Contrasting Servants (24:45-51)

The manager that fulfills his responsibilities will be found faithful when his boss unexpectedly drops in to observe him. Such a one would be rewarded. In contrast, the manager who thinks that his boss will not check up for a long time and abuses his subordinates and parties with drunkards will be caught in the act and judged (v. 51). The wise will learn from the example of the business world and be prepared for Messiah's return by actively fulfilling his responsibilities to Messiah, working as unto the Lord.

e. Parable of the Ten Virgins (25:1-13).

In the Jewish culture, proper preparation was necessary to

be a part of the torch light procession that escorted the groom and his bride to the wedding feast at the groom's home. When the groom was to arrive to take his bride home was not known. The wise virgins were those seeking to meet the groom and serve him, and, therefore they were able to enter the wedding feast. Prepared with sufficient oil, they met the groom, served their purpose, and entered the feast. The *foolish* virgins, unprepared, were unable to accompany the wedding procession. When they arrived late at the feast they were not recognized by the groom and were unable to enter. The wise will learn from the example of social life and be prepared for Messiah's return.

f. Parable of the Proper Way to Invest Money (25:14-30).

The kingdom of heaven, identified by the "it" in verse 14, is living in proper relationship with God while anticipating His return. Such living is here illustrated by proper investing of the earthly goods, talents, and silver money an owner entrusts to his investors. The investor who is prepared for the return of his account owner is one who has maximized the opportunity to obtain financial gain by accruing interest with the money. The unprepared investor is one who has misjudged the character of the account owner and has not taken advantage of his investment opportunities. In this parable, two investors fulfilled their responsibilities and were rewarded. Both good investors received the same praise, "You were faithful with a few things, I will put you in charge of many things (vv. 21, 23). This resulted even though one was gifted with less to invest than the other. The third person trusted with the owner's goods was rebuked as a "wicked, lazy" servant. He lost the privilege of investing for the owner and was "cast into the outer darkness." For that reason we, too, should be ready (v. 44). How Messiah will deal with people on His return is similar to how an owner deals with an incompetent investor of his goods.

Points to ponder from the parable: (1) God is the owner of the talents (i.e., our possessions are merely loaned to us by the true owner for His service); (2) we are held responsible for possessions and opportunities we *possess,* not for those we *do not possess;* and (3) the point of the parable is that two servants acknowledged the character of their Master and their responsibility to use gift and opportunity. This act of service for which they are rewarded is a result of their esteem for their Master. Note the contrast in the third servant. He refused to invest because of his analysis of his master's character as a hard man, unjust, "reaping were [he] did not sow and gathering where [he] scattered no seed" (v. 26). Afraid of losing the talent, he buried it. Was he lazy? Yes, he was rebuked for laziness and he misjudged the character of the one he served and consequently was unfaithful to him and was punished.

The conclusion in verses 29-30 applies the point of the parables to all of us. Those who use opportunities and possessions for God's good purposes will receive more of the same. But those who do not will lose what has already been given. Hyperbole is found in verse 30, unless the "worthless slave" is interpreted to be an unbeliever. Reasons for acknowledging him as an unbeliever are clear: he has *no* understanding of the character of God. You cannot love one you do not know. Love for God is a result of our recognizing His love for us. Recognition of His love for us "casts out all fear," sets us free so that we can serve Him with our possessions and opportunities.

g. Judgment of the Nations (25:31-46).

A few days before His crucifixion, Jesus stated that as the sovereign Messiah He will judge. This is the only time in the gospel of Matthew that Christ explicitly called Himself "the King." And here alone does He speak of Himself as the royal Judge. This particular passage is found only in Matthew (cf. Matt. 16:27; 19:28). The "nations" or national entities reflect the character of their constituents, and therefore, it is the individual constituents who will be judged. "Sheep" (v. 32) are those blessed of the Father because their works prove their faith, and they inherit the kingdom prepared "from the foundation of the world" (v. 34; cf. Eph. 1:4). In this kingdom, Christ will be recognized as the Sovereign, and the character of the participants will be a reflection of Him. The sheep's character shows compassion, service, and unselfishness: they provided physical help (clothing, medicine, food, and drink), social help (shelter and fellowship for strangers), and emotional help (v. 36, "I was in prison, and you came to Me"). A clue to the character of those who received help from the sheep is their close identification with Christ (vv. 35-36, 40). They are called "brethren of Mine" (v. 40). Also, because they appear to be present at the judgment (v. 40), they are probably among those believers who are with Him at the judgment of the nations (Dan. 7:22; 1 Cor. 6:2-4), saints of the most high God. But help is to be extended to all in need. In one sense, everyone, believer or unbeliever, who has a need that we have the ability to meet is a brother.

That the sheep were surprised that serving brethren in need was equated to serving Christ Himself (vv. 37-39) stresses the unselfishness of their motives. They had no idea they were serving the One they loved by serving the ones in need. No previous connection had been made between the sovereign Lord who would one day give rewards and the impoverished brethren who could give no reward. Their service was an unpretentious outflowing of a life of faith.

Equally surprised are the goats (v. 32), who conversely refused compassion to those in need, and by committing those sins of neglect showed their contempt for the character of Christ (vv. 41-45). Having had no relationship with the Author of unselfish love, they must experience an eternal destiny separated from a positive relationship with Him. Christ here disputed the teaching of annihilation. Although the lake of fire was not primarily made for man (v. 41), his rejection of Christ made his residence there a certainty (Matt. 5:22, 29-30; 18:8-9). Conversely, those related to Christ cannot be condemned (John 3:18; 5:24) and will receive the greatest of all blessings (Ps. 17:15; 73:23-25); they will live with Him eternally (v. 46).

Thus Christ ended His sixth discourse with both warning and consolation! The judgment described may be distinct from the final great white throne judgment (Rev. 20) and could take place after the Tribulation and before establishment of the millennial kingdom. Matthew, the gospel of the kingdom, has also been called the "gospel of judgment" (cf. Matt. 3:12; 6:2, 5, 16; 7:24-27; 13:30, 40-49; 18:23-34; 20:1-16; 21:33-41; 22:1-14; 24:45-51; 25:1-12, 13-30). Judgment precedes the establishment of the Kingdom (see also Dan. 9:14, 22-27).

13

THE KING'S PASSION

III. THE PASSION AND RESURRECTION OF THE KING (26:1—28:20)

Christ's public ministry and presentation to Israel was officially over. His disciples had been instructed concerning the rejection of Israel and the spiritual basis for entrance into the earthly kingdom. All that remained necessary to recount was the special ministry by which Messiah would provide the means of entrance into His kingdom. That special ministry of Messiah was His death and resurrection. Matthew leads us to His exalted conclusion by recounting the seeming defeat (humiliation and death) and then the glorious victory (resurrection) of his King.

A. PASSION OF THE KING (26:1—27:66)

A passion event is one in which deep emotions related to suffering occur. Matthew now takes us through the deepest suffering anyone could experience. From the prediction of His crucifixion two days hence, to His death, the depth of Christ's suffering grew, until those heinous yet blessed moments when the sin of the world was laid on His torn soul as He gave His life for us!

1. *Prediction of His Passion* (26:1-5)

Immediately following His statement about the Great Tribulation and eternal punishment, Christ again predicted His death (vv. 1-2). With the contrast between eternal life and eternal death as a background, Christ spoke of the factor that decides each person's fate—His crucifixion.

Probably while Christ spoke to His disciples, the Sanhedrin was meeting at the home of the high priest and plotting Jesus' death. Caiaphas, the high priest (A.D. 18-36), son-in-law and successor to Annas, sought Christ's death. Initially it was decided not to confront Christ during the Passover feast, for many of the people supported Him and could possibly cause a riot. But Christ, in divine prevision, knew that He must die as the Paschal Lamb during Passover.

2. *Messiah is Anointed for Burial* (26:6-13)

Jesus was at the home of Mary, Martha, and Lazarus in Bethany where He spent each night of this His last week. A feast in His honor, given by Simon (whom Jesus apparently healed of leprosy), probably the father of Martha, Lazarus, and Mary, is the scene for the anointing. The great value of the ointment (worth a year's wages, Mark 14:5) poured over Christ's head caused some of the disciples to question Mary's prudence. They felt the cost of the perfume could have better been used for the relief of the poor. Messiah taught that there may be an occasion when another ministry, because of its brief opportunity, may take precedence over feeding the poor. It is a misunderstanding of the text to teach that the church should not take responsibility for the poor because "the poor [we] will have with [us] always," no matter how hard we try to overcome poverty. Care for the poor is the perpetual obligation of the followers of Christ (Matt. 25:31-46).

3. *Judas Negotiates the Betrayal of Messiah* (26:14-16)

As a Zealot, Judas had hoped Christ would war against Rome. But with that possibility gone, he apparently attempted to get what he could from his relationship with Christ. The price of betrayal was the amount prophesied (Zech. 11:12-13). Matthew is the only gospel that names the demeaning price of the betrayal. Because Judas knew the Lord's habits (John 13:2), he was able to anticipate where Jesus might be found and arrested.

4. *Institution of the Lord's Supper* (26:17-35)

Messiah had desired to meet with His disciples for this last feast (Luke 22:15). Secrecy in choosing the location of the feast ensured privacy for His last uninterrupted session with the disciples before His crucifixion. The Lord told them He would be betrayed by one of the company. Each of the disciples asked if he was the betrayer. For the first and only time recorded in Matthew, Messiah is called Rabbi (teacher); Judas used that special title of respect prior to being privately identified as the betrayer. He could have avoided his eternal doom (v. 25) by recanting. The departure of Judas from the feast (John 13:30) is omitted by Matthew.

Because the lamb had to be slain at the Temple, every Passover feast celebrated at any location other than Jerusalem lacked the Passover lamb. Although this last feast was held in Jerusalem, no mention was made of the lamb. The thousands of lambs that had for centuries died as substitutes for the death of the Lamb of God sacrificed "from the foundations of the world" (Rev. 13:8) were no longer to be offered. Christ Himself would die and His death would be remembered by: (1) the breaking and eating of bread, depicting the breaking of His body and the resultant spiritual sustenance it provided to His church; and (2) the sharing of a cup of wine, which would remind His followers that with the shedding of His blood, His death sealed a contract, a new covenant (Jer. 31:31) between God the Father and those who would believe. The death of the precious Son of God would provide forgiveness for the penalty of sin.

This "supper memorial" will continue until the slain, resurrected Christ returns in glory and establishes His visible kingdom on earth (v. 29). The hymn (v. 30) is probably the traditional Passover Hallel of Psalms 115-118.

Apparently, after the conclusion of the supper and during the crossing of the Kidron Valley to the Mount of Olives, Christ made another prediction concerning His death. He made a slight change in the quote from Zechariah 13:7 and applied it to Himself, stating that He would be stricken down (i.e., killed), and that His disciples would forsake Him. His third prediction was that He would be "raised" (v. 32).

Peter refused to believe that he would forsake the Messiah (vv. 33, 35), and all the other disciples felt similarly confident. But Jesus singled out Peter, the leader, and predicted that he would deny Him three times before the cock would crow.

5. *Prayer in the Garden of Gethsemane* (26:36-46)

A quiet location amid a grove of olive trees called Gethsemane was where Christ often retired for private prayer (Luke 22:39-53) and where He now went. Eleven disciples were a distance away, but the three who witnessed the transfiguration—Peter, James, and John—were close with the Lord so that they might share His midnight agony in an intimate way. Even the Lord of glory in His humanity needed the support of others and communion in prayer with the Father as He faced this greatest of all ordeals. His sorrow was so deep in anticipation of bearing the penalty for the sin of the world that the resultant physical stress on His body could have killed Him.

The cup represented the Father's wrath against sin, which would be borne out in Christ's death on the cross with all the bitterness it contained (Isa. 51:22). His prayer was answered and grace was given to Him to bear the trial (Luke 22:43). Although the Messiah could not rejoice in His agony, He would bear it. Yet His three closest companions in careless weariness did not supply the needed sympathy to ease the loneliness and desolation so much a part of all sorrow and grief. Christ dedicated Himself absolutely to do the Father's will. His crying at this point is stressed in Hebrews 5:7. And, as always, the Father gave all of the grace necessary to do His will. Victory always comes when men humble themselves to the will of the Father.

6. *Messiah Is Taken Captive* (26:47-56)

As Christ anticipated, Judas came with the Temple police holding clubs and with Roman soldiers carrying their swords

(John 18:12, 48). The kiss by which Judas said he would identify Christ (v. 48) was the word used of a common means of
friendly greeting. But the word used to describe the actual *kiss*
or *kisses* when Judas kissed Christ (v. 49) is a more intense
word than in verse 48. Judas betrayed the Lord with en-
thusiasm and kissed Christ repeatedly. In return, Jesus addressed Judas as "friend," or a better translation would be
"companion" (v. 50).

Although Christ asked that His disciples be allowed to
leave, Peter chose to remain and attempted to defend his
Lord. With a sacrificial knife that he apparently swung as a
broad sword, Peter cut off the ear of Malchus, the servant of
the high priest (v. 51; John 18:10). However, Jesus intended
to submit to His enemies' humiliating seizure and rebuked
Peter's lack of discernment (vv. 52-54). His cause would not
be advanced by violence.

Had He chosen to do so, Christ could have commissioned
the help of legions of angels. In the Old Testament, one angel
had the power to slay 186,000 men in Sennacherib's Assyrian
army in one night (2 Kings 19:35). It is obvious that Peter's
help was unnecessary. Messiah had all the power and authority necessary to subdue His captors, but chose not to exercise
it. He came to fulfill divine prophecy and die (Isa. 53:12).

Messiah's rebuke of His captors (v. 55) revealed His total
control. He was fully conscious of His part in messianic
prophecy and totally confident of the veracity of the Old
Testament Scriptures. Jesus *allowed* Himself to be taken that
the Scriptures might be fulfilled (vv. 54, 56).

As prophesied in Zechariah 13:7, when His disciples saw
that they could not prevent His captivity, they fled.

7. *Jesus Is Judged in the House of the High Priest* (26:67-68)
From the Garden of Gethsemane Messiah was taken to the
house of Annas, the ex-high priest and power behind the
reigning religious party. There Christ was condemned to die
(John 18:12-14; 19-24). Matthew next picks up the narrative
when Christ was brought before Caiaphas, the reigning high

priest and the Sanhedrin, the religious supreme court. These first two "trials" were illegal for many reasons according to Jewish law expressed in the Mishna. First, a man could not be tried for his life at night; Christ was condemned between one and three o'clock A.M. Second, a capital crime could not be heard on the eve of a major feast, such as Passover. Third, the accused could not be asked to incriminate himself. Fourth, a minimum of twenty-four hours was required to transpire between the initial conviction and the review of the case and sentencing. But the high priest was a master at casuistry and circumventing regulations. The decision was actually prearranged (John 11:49-52).

Peter, trying to remain true to his promise never to forsake the Master, followed the throng as it moved from the home of Annas to the home of Caiaphas. There an attempt was made to obtain false testimony by which Christ could be "legally" condemned in accordance with the previously arraigned verdict. No agreement could be found among the witnesses as they individually lied against Him. Then it was remembered that Jesus claimed He would raise up the Temple after it was destroyed (v. 61). They misquoted Him and accused Him of claiming He would destroy the Temple and then raise it up (cf. John 2:19). To destroy the Temple would be to desecrate it. But the raising of the Temple was an allusion to Christ's resurrection, the Temple representing His body (John 2:21). When Caiaphas demanded that He respond to the accusation, Jesus kept silent in fulfillment of prophecy (Isa. 53:7). Christ had come to die as a lamb and would not defend Himself.

In apparent frustration, the high priest directly asked Jesus if He was the Christ, the Son of God. For the first time recorded in Matthew, Jesus stated publicly and clearly that He was indeed the Messiah, the Son of God (v. 64). "You have said it" means, "Yes I am," or "Yes indeed," and is very similar to the phrase found in Matthew 27:11. Paul spoke of that as a "good confession before Pontius Pilate" (1 Tim. 6:13). In quoting and applying Daniel 7:13 to Himself, Jesus was saying that as the Son of God, He *is* God, and the time was coming when He would ultimately have glory.

If Christ were not the fulfillment of Daniel 7:13, then He had blasphemed, He had injured the character of God by claiming that God was like Him. Such blasphemy was worthy of death (Lev. 24:15-16). Upon hearing that confession, the high priest was socially obligated to show his grief by tearing his robes. In doing so, he apparently violated Leviticus 21:10. Caiaphas believed he had found the cause for death he had so earnestly sought. His "grief" was probably an act. There was no longer a need for other "witnesses." The court had heard Him blaspheme. It was nearly 3 A.M. and everybody could finally go home. The verdict was unanimous among those who were there (Mark 14:64). Apparently, Joseph of Arimathea was absent (Luke 23:50-51).

The Temple police and palace guards fulfilled prophecy (Isa. 50:6; 52:14) as they blasphemed the Son of God, hitting, spitting on, and most cruelly of all, mocking Him. They blindfolded Christ (Luke 22:64) and then challenged Him, as the Christ, to identify His attackers (v. 68).

8. *Peter's Denial* (26:69-75)

Peter had sincerely but self-confidently argued that he would never forsake the Lord (Matt. 26:33-35). But He was by nature a fearful man (Luke 5:10) and, like others of similar commitment to God, was prone to fail when physically, emotionally, or spiritually exhausted. Peter's failure came after a long, strenuous night of sorrow and bewilderment. Even Elijah doubted after an exhausting experience with the prophets of Baal, as did Jonah after the series of strenuous events that led to the success of his preaching to Nineveh.

The "you too" of verse 69 links Peter with the apostle John. John, known by the Temple guards as a follower of Christ, apparently requested that Peter be allowed into the courtyard (John 18:15-16).

Peter's first denial was a formal statement such as would be made before a court. Before he had a chance to leave, another servant girl suggested that he was a follower of Christ. That second denial was more emotional and accompanied by an oath. About an hour later, as Peter tried to lose himself in the crowd (Luke 22:59), apparently a relative of Malchus (John 18:26) recognized him. Peter called down on himself condemnation, a "curse" if he was lying about not knowing the Lord. Immediately, the cock crowed and thereby fulfilled Christ's prophecy (Matt. 26:34). At that very moment Messiah, being led from the judgment hall through the courtyard to the soldier's barracks, caught Peter's eye (Luke 22:61). Instantly Peter remembered the prophecy, and conviction of his unfaithfulness brought him to bitter sorrow and repentance.

9. *Messiah Is Judged by Rome* (27:1-26)

To wait the full twenty-four hours to review the case and pronounce sentence was politically inappropriate because it would give Christ's supporters a chance to mount opposition. Therefore, shortly after daybreak the Sanhedrin met again to give a semblance of legality to its preceedings. The decision to put Christ to death was quickly reaffirmed. The Jewish people were not allowed to inflict capital punishment, so Messiah was taken to Pontius Pilate, the Roman governor, so that the execution might be performed (vv. 1-2).

Matthew is the only gospel that records Judas' death (vv. 3-10). Judas observed Christ's condemnation and then felt remorseful for what he had done (v. 3). His "repentance" was not a change of mind about who Jesus really was, and it was not a decision to put his trust in Him as Messiah (Matt. 3:2; 4:17; Acts 2:38, 3:19). Judas may have regretted being part of a contrived act that had condemned a good man to death, but he was annoyed by the *consequences* of what he had done rather than being concerned with the *cause* that had motivated his act. This political zealot, influenced by a love for money (John 12:6), had rejected the One who said that "man shall not live by bread alone" (Matt. 4:4). Judas knew that his attempt to make amends by giving back the money would not quiet his conscience and, with nowhere to turn for forgiveness, he planned to take his own life.

The religious leaders (v. 4) were unsympathetic toward Judas and refused to allow the blood money in their Temple treasury. In anger, Judas threw the money into the holy place open only to priests.

Distinctions in Matthew's account of Judas' death, when harmonized with Luke's account in Acts 1:18-19, may indicate that Judas hung himself on a tree that reached out over a cliff. When the rope or branch finally broke, he fell to the ground below.

Since the blood money of Judas would defile the Temple treasury (Deut. 23:18), it could not be used for anything that related to the Temple. It was decided to use the silver to buy a burial place for strangers who died in Jerusalem. The potter's field or "acre of ceramics," was probably a field from which potters got their clay. When the clay in the field was used up, the field was offered for sale. The price of betrayal for the Friend of the poor would be used to buy a place for their burial. But that attempt at a good deed could not cover up the source of the money: the inhabitants of the area would henceforth call the potters' field the "Field of Blood."

Matthew attributes the prophecy of verses 8 and 10 to Jeremiah, possibly because Jeremiah was sometimes the first book in the section called the Prophets, from which part of this allusion comes. However, it could be because he has combined two references together and attributed the combined quote to the more prominent of the prophets. Similarly, the quote found in 2 Chronicles 36:21 is drawn from Leviticus 26:34-35 and Jeremiah 25:12, but is ascribed only to Jeremiah.

Jeremiah speaks of a plot of ground used for burial purposes that would come to be known as the "field of blood" or "valley of slaughter" because of the shedding of innocent blood (Jer. 19:1, 3, 6, 11). Also, in Jeremiah 32:7-15 Jeremiah bought a field.

In Zechariah 11:12-13, from where the rest of the prophecy

is taken, we read how Zechariah's prophetic ministry as a prophet-shepherd to Judah was held in contempt by the people. They considered his ministry worth only thirty pieces of silver, the price of a slave (Ex. 21:32). The Lord told Zechariah to throw the money to the potter (one of the lowest laboring classes), which would be equivalent to "throwing it away."[1] A variant reading for "potter" (KJV)* is "treasury" (RSV)† so that the chief priest in Matthew's account may have been asking his cohorts which interpretation they wanted to follow: Should they put the money in the treasury or throw it to the potter?

Does it not inspire awe in us to know that both the death of the betrayer and the use of the price for the betrayal were both prophesied? Would we not be frightened to know of God's intrinsic involvement in Scripture and all of life but for our knowledge of His grace through our Messiah?

At the time of those trials, Pontius Pilate was being critically observed by Roman officials. Within three years that cruel and unstable governor of Judea would be recalled from his political position. The Jews had already rioted several times because of his policies.

Pilate knew that to protect his position he needed to keep peace in the Holy City. During the Passover season Jerusalem's population would so swell that the danger of a full scale rebellion existed and could be sparked by just such a situation as he faced.

The Jews knew that Rome would not crucify a man merely because he blasphemed against the Hebrew God (Matt. 26:65), so they changed the charge to treason; Christ had claimed to be the king of the Jews (Luke 23:1-2) and was a threat to the emperor, Tiberius. But when questioned, Jesus stated that His kingdom was not of this world, and Pilate

*King James Version.
†Revised Standard Version.

1. A. Cohen. *The Soncino Chumash* (London: Soncino, 1964), 14:316.

concluded that Jesus was not guilty of any crime worthy of death (John 18:26-38).

Still, the religious leaders insisted that Jesus was a criminal guilty of causing trouble from Galilee to Judea (Luke 23:5). Herod Antipas, governor of Galilee, was in Jerusalem for the holidays, so Pilate sent Christ to Herod for judgment. Herod interrogated Christ, mocked Him, and returned Him to Pilate with the verdict that Christ was not guilty (Luke 23:6-12).

Pilate customarily released a Jewish prisoner during Passover, a symbolic gesture toward the Jewish celebration of deliverance. He knew that the leaders were jealous of Christ (v. 18) and that the people five days earlier had sung praises to Him as He entered the city (v. 18). Pilate assumed that if given the choice, the people would choose that Christ be the prisoner set free.

But while the governor was called from the porch to listen to his wife's exclamation of her vivid dream about Christ, the leaders apparently convinced the crowd to choose the release of Barabbas, the murderer and traitor to Rome. The unjust prisoner was to be released that the just prisoner might die in his place.

The crowd began to riot when Pilate asked what Christ had done. When they called for Messiah to be crucified, Pilate symbolically washed his hands of any responsibility, attempting to shift blame for himself to the people and their leaders (v. 20; cf. Deut. 21:6-8; Ps. 73:13).

"All the people," (v. 25) refers to those present. Some of the leaders and others opposed the crucifixion (Luke 23:24, 51). In essence we are all responsible for Christ's crucifixion (Rom. 5:8).

In a last attempt to win sympathy for Jesus and change the mind of the people, Pilate had Christ flogged (v. 26). Christ had already been beaten with fists and spat upon (v. 30; Matt. 26:67; Mark 14:65). That whipping, reserved for murderers and traitors, was so cruel that a lesser man would have died. The thongs of the whip were imbedded with sharpened pieces of bone or metal. Flesh was often laid bare to the inner organs and prisoners frequently died from the floggings. Only the great physical strength of Christ and His will to live until He had endured the cross kept Him alive.

In Isaiah 52 and 53 we read the graphic descriptions of how Christ fulfilled the prophecies of Isaiah by suffering and dying for us: "His appearance was marred more than any man, and His form more than the sons of men" (Isa. 52:14). "He was pierced through for our transgressions, He was crushed for our iniquities . . . He was oppressed and He was afflicted" (Isa. 53:5, 7). Those prophecies so surely spoke of the coming Messiah that up until the eleventh century B.C. no rabbi seriously tried to raise an alternative interpretation.[2]

10. *The Way to the Cross* (27:27-32)

Jesus was taken from the porch of the Fort of Antonia, the Praetorium (or governor's home) and quarters where Pilate had conversed with the Jews, to the courtyard. There three to six hundred soldiers mocked him, stripped Him of His clothing, and for the second time placed a scarlet military cloak on Him (v. 28; Luke 23:11). They crowned Him, spit in His face, beat Him with a reed, proclaimed Him king of the Jews, and derisively genuflected.

The crown of thorns was probably made of a species of the date-palm that had spikes sometimes twelve inches in length. Thorns are an evidence of God's curse on nature resulting from the Fall (Gen. 3:18). Here we see Christ symbolically bearing the curse on nature that one day He might deliver nature from it.

A prisoner was not to be put to death within the city walls, so Jesus was taken outside the city to be crucified. Usually, the condemned criminal was made to carry his own cross. But the repeated beatings, the flogging, and stresses of the previous twelve hours had drained Christ of His strength. Simon, a Jew or Jewish proselyte from Cyrene, the capital of

---

2. Arnold Fruchtenbaum. *Jesus Was a Jew* (Nashville: Broadman, 1974), 31-32.

Cyrenaica in North Africa, was forced to carry the cross. Apparently, Simon stayed to observe the crucifixion and then became a believer in Christ, for he, his wife, and sons became known among the believers (Mark 15:21; Rom. 16:13).

11. *The Crucifixion* (27:33-56)

Crucifixions were conducted at Golgotha (Aramaic for "skull"), also known as Calvary (its Latin name). The location probably got its name from its appearance, which resembled a skull. Wealthy women of Jerusalem had provided a narcotic for the condemned men that would dull pain and possibly induce a more rapid death (cf. Ps. 69:21). When offered the wine mixed with gall by the soldiers, Christ refused it. He came into this world to die for our sins and was determined to retain a clear mind until His work was finished.

Nails were driven through His hands and feet (John 20:25; Luke 23:39-40), and the accusation sign "THIS IS THE KING OF THE JEWS," shown by Matthew to be true, was affixed over His head. The statement was written in three languages. When the base of the cross was dropped into a three-foot-deep hole and brought up straight, sufficient pressure to pull bones from their joints was brought to bear. Because the primary purpose of Christ's death was to pay for our sins, little emphasis was put on His great physical suffering (v. 46; cf. Isa. 53:10; John 10:11, 15). The soldiers were posted to ensure that no one mutilated or tried to free the prisoners.

The two robbers, probably cohorts of Barabbas, crucified on either side of Christ (vv. 38, 43), initially threw insults at Him. But in response to Christ's demeanor and words, one of the robbers became convinced that Christ was who He said He was and committed his life to Him (Luke 23:39-43).

The crosses were planted by the roadside so that passersby could observe and be warned. The derisive insults addressed to Christ reflected one or more of His claims (vv. 40-41, 43). The very words used by Satan in the temptation in the wilderness are used here (cf. Matt. 4:6): "If you are the Son of God," come down from the cross. However, it was because He *was* the Son of God that He would not come down from the cross. He was to die for the very sin of their insults. This derision fulfills Psalm 22:7-18.

From 9 A.M. until noon the area was dark. It was as if God the Father had pulled a veil over the eyes of those who would look upon the spiritual suffering of His beloved Son (v. 45). At the moment when the sin of the world was laid upon Jesus, spiritual fellowship with the Father and with the Holy Spirit was broken, and Messiah cried out in agony, "My God, My God, why hast Thou forsaken me" (v. 46). "He made Him who knew no sin to be sin on our behalf" (2 Cor. 5:21). The spiritual agony of those moments made Jesus' physical suffering a secondary factor. The words of Christ (v. 46) were a fulfillment of Psalm 22:1. Some bystanders misunderstood what Christ said and thought He was calling for the help of Elijah (v. 49). It was believed by many that Elijah, who had not died but had been translated, would come to the aid of those who called upon him in time of need.

The sour wine (or vinegar) offered on a sponge fulfilled the latter part of the prediction of Psalm 69:21. With His work of bearing our sins completed, Jesus cried out, "It is finished" (v. 50; John 19:30). He then voluntarily "yielded up His spirit." His life was not taken from Him, but at the proper moment, after having been made "a curse for us" that we might be redeemed from the "curse of the Law" (Gal. 3:13), He gave up His physical life (v. 50). Messiah was in control of His life to the end.

At the very moment of His death, that which all Old Testament blood sacrifices had anticipated was fulfilled. No longer would it be necessary for a representative of Israel to enter the Holy of Holies and sprinkle blood on the Mercy Seat to cover annually the sins of the nation. Neither would personal animal sacrifices be necessary any longer. Christ had once and for all paid the price for all sin and opened the way for all those who trust Him to enter the very throne room of God. Sin, previously covered, was now blotted out (Col. 2:14).

What had been true from the Fall of the first Adam to the death of the second Adam was now clear: faith in Messiah is the key to eternal life with God. Rejection of Messiah is the only factor that keeps man from an eternity with Him.

To show symbolically that direct access to God was available to all humankind, the veil that separated the holy place from the Holy of Holies (where the invisible presence of the God of Israel was enthroned) was torn from top to bottom. Any and all with true faith could enter God's presence (Heb. 6:19-20; 10:19-22). That veil embroidered with cherubim measured 60 feet by 30 feet and took 300 men to lift.

At the moment of the cry of Christ (v. 50) and the tearing of the veil, two other events occurred: an earthquake (v. 51) and the restoration of physical life to believers who had died (vv. 52-53). The latter event symbolized Christ's victory over death ("death is swallowed up in victory," 1 Cor. 15:54). Christ's death affected the world of the dead over whom He would also rule (Phil. 2:10-11).

Amid those visible manifestations, the pragmatic, nonreligious Roman centurion and his companions were apparently brought to faith: "Truly this was the Son of God!" (v. 54). With their confession they joined the religious pilgrim, Simon, and the condemned thief.

Some of the women who followed Christ watched the crucifixion. They demonstrated compassion and courage above that of all the apostles except John. Several of those women are identified (vv. 55-56; see also Matt. 20:20; 27:61; 28:1; Mark 15:40; Luke 8:2; John 19:25).

12. *The Burial of Messiah* (27:57-61)

"And when it was evening" (v. 57) a wealthy man named Joseph requested from Pilate the privilege of burying the body of Jesus (vv. 57-58). The centurion assured Pilate that Jesus was dead and the body was released to him (Mark 15:45).

The Jewish day consisted of two evenings, early evening

beginning at 3 P.M., and the second evening at 6 P.M.[3] The body had to be buried before 6 P.M., when the most important Sabbath of the year would begin. It was against the Mosaic law to leave a body on a "tree" overnight (Deut. 21:23; Gal. 3:13). All of the apostles had fled but John, and he was busy going to and from his home taking care of Jesus' mother (John 19:27, 35) and had no time to prepare for the burial of his Lord.

Joseph was from Arimathea, a location about twenty miles northwest of Jerusalem. He was a good man, righteous, and a member of the Sanhedrin (Mark 15:43; Luke 23:51). He had been a secret follower of Christ (John 19:38), but now, in time of special need, he came forward and bravely acted on the Lord's behalf. It was customary for a wealthy man to prepare his place of burial long before his death, and thus was fulfilled the prophecy of Isaiah 53:9, "His grave was assigned . . . with a rich man in His death." The clean linen cloth in which the body was wrapped was similar to the cloth in which Christ was wrapped as a baby (v. 59; Luke 2:7)—He had been born to die. John tells us that Nicodemus joined Joseph at the tomb with about 100 pounds of spices and ointment (John 19:38-42; see also Mark 15:42-47). Aloe was a fragrant wood pounded into dust, and myrrh was an aromatic gum that would be mixed with it.[4] A semiliquid unguent such as nard was usually added to the other ingredients to help them adhere to the body.

Two of the Marys who had observed the crucifixion also observed the burial. They would return the next day for another anointing of the body and attest that the tomb where He had been laid was empty. As Wilbur Smith stated, "We know more about the burial of the Lord Jesus than we know

3. William Hendriksen. *Exposition of the Gospel of Matthew* (Grand Rapids: Baker, 1975), 979.
4. Josh McDowell. *Evidence That Demands a Verdict* (Arrowhead Springs, Calif.: Campus Crusade, 1972), 213.

of the burial of any single character in all of ancient history."[5]

A stone was pushed in front of the entrance to this sepulcher to guard against body snatchers.

13. *Securing Messiah's Tomb* (27:62-66)

"On the next day" (Saturday), possibly before the Sabbath was over, the Sadducees and Pharisees joined forces and went to Pilate to ask for help (v. 62). They were aware that Christ had prophesied He would arise from the grave in three days (v. 63), and although they did not believe that He could come back to life, they feared that His disciples might steal His body and pretend He had been resurrected. Their hope was to get Pilate's help to secure the entrance of the tomb beyond human tampering (v. 64).

Guards were posted, probably four men on each of the eight-hour shifts (v. 65). The seal was usually a wax-covered cord connecting the stone and the side of the rock tomb. The cord was impressed with the seal of Rome so that any efforts to tamper with the entrance would be detected. To tamper with the official seal was a crime worthy of death.

The guards were probably Roman soldiers, possibly some of those who had guarded the crucifixion. They feared Pilate more than the Temple authorities (Matt. 28:11, 14), which would not be the case if they had been Temple police. The penalty for a Roman soldier quitting his post was death! Discipline for dereliction of duty was swift and severe. Temple police were beaten or their garments set on fire if they fell asleep on the job (Rev. 16:15). Everything that could humanly be done to prevent a resurrection was set in place.

5. Wilbur M. Smith. "Scientists and the Resurrection." *Christianity Today,* April 15, 1957, 370-71.

14

THE KING'S RESURRECTION

B. THE RESURRECTION OF THE KING (28:1-20)

Human design cannot hinder the plan of God. As predicted, Messiah was resurrected from the grave. No record of that event is more majestic than Matthew's. Yet, Matthew's record is not a strict chronological account of the events on and around resurrection day. Resurrection life transcends time! Neither is his account a detailed description of the events of the first Christian Sunday. Matthew limits his record to the story of two women, an angel, the guards, and eleven disciples. Mark 16:1-8, Luke 14:1-12, John 20:1-31, and 1 Corinthians 15:1-11 add other details.

1. *The Two Marys Meet the Resurrected Christ* (28:1-10)

Matthew summarizes the visit of the women to the tomb by concentrating on Mary Magdalene and the "other Mary" (the mother of James and Joseph, Matt. 27:56, 61). Linen mixed with myrrh and aloes had already been wound around the body, but the women hoped to apply a second anointing (Mark 16:1; Luke 24:1).

Before they arrived at the tomb, a "severe earthquake" occurred. Also, an angel already had descended from heaven, rolled back the stone, turned it over, and sat on it. Luke 24:1 and John 20:12 record a second angel. Earthquakes occurred at His crucifixion (Matt. 27:51), at His resurrection (Matt. 28:2), and will occur at His second coming (Matt. 24:7; Zech. 14:4). God was telling the world to stop and listen (cf. Ex. 19:18).

The appearance of the angel struck fear in the hearts of the guards, and they "shook" (literally, quaked) like the earth before they either fainted or were knocked unconscious. When they regained consciousness they fled before the women arrived (vv. 11-15).

When the women arrived and saw the angel, they too were frightened. But unlike the soldiers, they were told not to be afraid. Those who trust Him need not fear His messengers. The angel knew of their courage and loyalty to Christ. To the women he announced the heart of the good news and the fantastic truth: "Jesus . . . crucified . . . risen" (vv. 5-6). Invited into the tomb, the women observed where Christ had been. Where His body had laid were the grave clothes, in the form of a cocoon (John 20:5-8), with the face cloth set aside. That would not have been possible had the grave been robbed or the body stolen. It appeared that Jesus had *passed through* the grave clothes!

Again the angel told the women that Christ had arisen (v. 7) and that they were to tell His disciples that they would see Him in Galilee (cf. Matt. 26:32). As the women ran from the tomb their fear was gradually and consciously overcome by "great joy" (v. 8).

Before they could reach the disciples, Jesus appeared to the women (v. 9). Their loyalty and courage were magnificiently rewarded. The degree to which those women loved and ministered to the Lord during His earthly days is recorded only in the heart of God. A king or prince was paid homage by his subjects by their falling before him and symbolically grasping his feet. That outward sign of reverence shown by those women toward Christ was augmented by their inward worship of Him. Worship of any one other than God Himself is forbidden by Scripture (Deut. 6:13; 10:20). Jesus explicitly stated that only God was to be worshiped (Matt. 4:10). But here Jesus Christ the Messiah accepted worship, for He was God (v. 9). The message that He gave the women is similar to that given by the angels, except that Jesus told them to take the word of His resurrection to His "brethren," instead of His "disciples" (v. 7) and to leave for Galilee (v. 10). Possibly

Jesus had in mind more people than His immediate eleven disciples. We know that before His resurrection His half-brothers did not believe in Him. But after His resurrection He appeared to them and they believed (1 Cor. 15:7; Acts 1:14). The assertion that He would meet His "brethren" in Galilee did not discount other meetings both before and after the Galilee meeting.

Neither the stone, the seal, the guards, the grave wrappings, nor death could stay the glorious plan of God. He was raised up, *just as He had said!* (cf. Matt. 16:21; 17:23; 20:19). God "laughs" at the attempts of man to stand in the way of His program of redemption (Ps. 2:4).

2. *The Soldiers Spread a False Rumor* (28:11-15)

While the women ran to spread the great truth, the soldiers were encouraged to spread a lie. For the sake of his Jewish readers who would be familiar with the rumor, Matthew includes the facts of its historical basis.

The elders, regional leaders from outlying Jewish communities, and the chief priest, made up two of the groups of the great Sanhedrin. They paid a "large sum of money" (v. 12) to bribe the guards to go along with their lie that the body was stolen. The guards agreed to the fabrication even though it made them appear guilty of dereliction of duty. Surely those soldiers would not have agreed had the religious leaders not already shown their ability, at least in this matter, to bend Pilate to their will and protect themselves from his wrath (Matt. 27:23-26). With the assurance of impunity (v. 14) the guards circulated an empty story that was passed on to the time of the writing of Matthew's gospel (v. 15) and even to this day (e.g., Hugh Schonfield, *The Passover Plot,* and Edwin Yamauchi's answer to Schonfield in "The Passover Ploy.")[1]

Because the guards could have been put to death for sleep-

---

1. Edwin Yamauchi. "The Passover Ploy," *Christianity Today,* March 17, 1967, 38-39.

ing on duty, it is ridiculous to think the disciples (who were too frightened to even witness the crucifixion) would or could steal the body from a contingent of armed soldiers (v. 13). Also, if the soldiers slept, how could they have known what happened? If the fearful and depressed disciples had attempted to steal the body, most likely they would have been heard as the seal was broken and the stone moved.

The gospel account of the resurrection of Jesus is both historically and intellectually reasonable. Early Christians believed in His resurrection, not because they did not find His body in the tomb, but because they found Him—alive and well!

3. *The Great Commission* (28:16-20)

As Christ promised, He met His disciples in Galilee where most of His public ministry had taken place. Those dwelling in darkness did indeed see a great light. Here Matthew brings us to the climax of His gospel.

Historically it has been assumed that the mount on which that meeting took place was the mount of transfiguration (Matt. 17:1) and the place where He had "appointed them" (Matt. 10:5-42). Many other significant events in Jesus' life took place on mountains in that region (Matt. 5:1; 14:23; 15:29; 17:1).

About a dozen resurrection appearances of Christ are recorded in Scripture. Possibly the account here is the same one recorded in 1 Corinthians 15:6, where Jesus made an appearance to the "five hundred brethren" the majority of whom were still alive when Paul wrote.

They worshiped the resurrected Savior. Worship of the Son of God, the Christian's highest occupation, always results in effective service.

Some (v. 17), possibly some of the five hundred, were or had been doubtful of the fact of His resurrection. Even the eleven doubted (Luke 24:10-11), with Thomas being the last to become convinced (John 20:24-29). In this instance it may have been that some merely doubted that the figure approaching them from a distance was Jesus. As He came closer, they were able to see that it was indeed He (v. 18).

All authority, power, and control over all that exists are His (v. 18; cf. 16:28; 24:30; 26:64; Dan. 7:14). Jesus Christ the Messiah is the focal point by which all of creation is held together (Col. 1:15-17). As God, He is eternally omnipotent. But during His sojourn on earth, He veiled His authority and voluntarily limited His power. Now, all authority is His as the God-man: "For to this end Christ died and lived again, that He might be Lord both of the dead and of the living" (Rom. 14:9; cf. Eph. 1:18-23; Phil. 2:9-18; Col. 2:10).

Matthew has shown in this gospel how Jesus' authority as the God-man grew from the dependent baby in the manger to the rebuker of false religion; healer of the blind, the lame, and the sin-scarred; the controller of His own death and resurrection; and, the owner-controller of all existence.

On the basis of His ownership and authority over all that exists, Messiah told His disciples to "go" and make disciples of all nations. That was an order! The phrase "make disciples" stresses understanding (i.e., the use of the mind) more than does the phrase "make converts." A disciple is a lifelong pupil or learner (Matt. 13:52; 24:14; John 8:31).

No longer was the disciples' mission to be restricted to the "lost sheep of the house of Israel" as it was during the Galilean ministry (Matt. 10:5-6). The keepers of God's revelation, the Jewish people, now had co-responsibility with the Gentiles.

The primary command, "make disciples," is further delineated by "baptizing," and "teaching them" (vv. 19-20). The baptizing must be done in the name of (note the singular, one name, hence one God), "The Father and the Son and the Holy Spirit." A name represents the one who bears it. To be baptized in the name of someone means to be brought into a vital relationship with that one as he has revealed himself."[2]

---

2. William Hendriksen. *Exposition of the Gospel of Matthew* (Grand Rapids: Baker, 1975), 1000.

The Trinitarian formula was especially appropriate for Gentiles who had turned to God from idols.[3] Spirit baptism having taken place, physical water baptism would be a public sign that the new disciples had personally committed their lives to Christ. As they learned of Messiah's ways they would voluntarily submit to baptism. "Jewish converts and others who already worshipped the living and true God were called to believe that Jesus was the Messiah and were therefore baptized specifically into His name (Acts 2:38; 8:16)."[4]

New disciples were to be taught to observe all that He had commanded them (v. 20). The "great light" seen by the Galileans and others was to spread across the earth.

Matthew concludes his gospel with the thought that the story was not over and that His followers can be wonderfully encouraged: Messiah did much more than tell His disciples how to live and what to believe; He guaranteed the literal focal point of His presence with them in the pursuit of His mission. The One whom you serve, if He be Jesus Christ, will be *with you* to empower your service with His presence. "I am with you always, even to the end of the age" (v. 20). The task that Messiah set before His disciples was beyond mere human ability. But God never asks anything of a man that He does not give him the power to fulfill. Disciples are ultimately subject to the ultimate Authority and are, therefore, not to fear the lesser powers of this world that may hinder in time, but will be as nothing in eternity.

3. F. F. Bruce. *St. Matthew* (Grand Rapids: Eerdmans, 1970), 94.
4. Ibid., 94-95.

BIBLIOGRAPHY

Barclay, William. *The Gospel of Matthew.* Philadelphia: Westminster, 1958.

Baxter, J. Sidlow. *Inter-Testament and the Gospels.* Vol. 5, *Explore the Book.* London: Marshall, Morgan, & Scott, 1975.

Bruce, F. F. *St. Matthew.* Grand Rapids: Eerdmans, 1970.

Cohen, A. *The Soncino Chumash.* London: Soncino, 1964.

Dana, H. E., and Mantey, Julius R. *A Manual Grammar of the Greek New Testament.* New York: MacMillan, 1959.

Eerdman, Charles R. *Matthew.* Philadelphia: Westminster, 1966.

Fruchtenbaum, Arnold. *Jesus Was a Jew.* Nashville: Broadman, 1974.

Hendriksen, William. *Exposition of the Gospel of Matthew.* Grand Rapids: Baker, 1975.

Hoehner, William. *Chronological Aspects of the Life of Christ.* Grand Rapids: Zondervan, 1978.

Johnson, S. Lewis, Jr. *The Old Testament in the New.* Grand Rapids: Zondervan, 1980.

Kent, Homer A., Jr. "Matthew." In *The Wycliffe Bible Commentary.* Chicago: Moody, 1962.

Lockyer, Herbert. *All the Messianic Prophecies of the Bible.* Grand Rapids: Zondervan, 1973.

McDowell, Josh. *Evidence That Demands a Verdict.* Arrowhead Springs, Calif.: Campus Crusade, 1972.

Nixon, R. E. "Matthew." In *The New Bible Commentary.* Rev. ed. Edited by D. Guthrie, J. A. Moyer, A. M. Stibbs, and D. J. Wiseman. Grand Rapids: Eerdmans, 1970.

Robertson, A. T. *Word Pictures in the New Testament.* Vol. 1, *Matthew.* Nashville: Broadman, 1930.

Ryrie, Charles C. *The Ryrie Study Bible* (NASB). Chicago: Moody, 1976.

Sanders, J. Oswald. *Bible Studies in Matthew's Gospel.* Grand Rapids: Zondervan, 1975.

Scroggie, W. Graham. *A Guide to the Gospels.* London: Pickering & Inglis, 1948.

Smith, Wilbur M. "Scientists and the Resurrection." *Christianity Today,* April 15, 1957, 370-71.

Slotki, Israel W. *Israel with Hebrew Text and English Translation.* London: Soncino, 1964.

Tasker, R. V. G. *The Gospel According to St. Matthew.* Grand Rapids: Eerdmans, 1976.

Tenney, Merrill C. *The New Testament: An Historical and Analytic Survey.* Grand Rapids: Eerdmans, 1960.

Unger, Merrill F. *Archeology and the New Testament.* Grand Rapids: Zondervan, 1962.

Vincent, Marvin R. *Word Studies in the New Testament.* Vol. 1. Grand Rapids: Eerdmans, 1946.

Vine, W. E. *An Expository Dictionary of New Testament Words.* London: Olipants, 1958.

Vos, Howard F. *Matthew: A Study Guide Commentary.* Grand Rapids: Zondervan, 1979.

Yamauchi, Edwin. "The Passover Ploy." *Christianity Today,* March 17, 1967, 38-39.

Zodhiates, Spiros. *The Pursuit of Happiness.* Grand Rapids: Eerdmans, 1966.

Moody Press, a ministry of the Moody Bible Institute, is designed for education, evangelization, and edification. If we may assist you in knowing more about Christ and the Christian life, please write us without obligation: Moody Press, c/o MLM, Chicago, Illinois 60610.